FORMING CHRISTIAN DISCIPLES

The Role of Covenant Discipleship and Class Leaders in the Congregation

David Lowes Watson

DISCIPLESHIP RESOURCES
MATERIALS FOR GROWTH IN CHRISTIAN FAITH AND LIFE
P.O. Box 189 • Nashville, TN 37202 • Phone (615) 340-7284

Cover design by Claudia Williams.

ISBN 0-88177-093-0

Library of Congress Card Catalog No. 90-82204

DR093B

In deep gratitude to
Hexham Road Methodist Church,
Throckley, England,
and
Grace United Methodist Church,
East St. Louis, Illinois,
for their Methodist tradition
of lay leadership.

Contents

end, 81; The Friday Evening Meal, 81; The Saturday Seminar and Role Play, 82; Resources for the Seminar, 83; The Saturday Evening, 83; The Sunday Worship Service, 84; The Invitation to Join a Group, 84; A Sample Covenant of Discipleship, 85; The Prayer of Commitment, 86; An Open Invitation, 87.

Part Three: Class Leaders in the Congregation

From Sect to Church, 129; From Leader to Sub-Pastor, 130; Frustrated Leadership, 131; Leaders in Discipleship, 132; Methodism Full Circle, 132; Hesitation to Share Leadership, 133; Essentials and Nonessentials, 133; Waiting to Be Asked, 134.

Acknowledgments

This handbook marks the transition of covenant discipleship from an initiative of the General Board of Discipleship to a firm place in the connectional work of The United Methodist Church. There are many people to be thanked for this development, but most especially the hundreds of congregational leaders, clergy and lay, who have formed covenant discipleship groups and given them priority in the ministry and mission of the church.

This book also marks an important step toward the recovery of the office of class leader, which in 1988 was restored to *The Book of Discipline of The United Methodist Church* for the first time in fifty years. The legislation for this, and for the revitalization of class meetings, was proposed by the Northern New Jersey Annual Conference, and drafted by Dr. Hae-Jong Kim. It was an appropriate and highly symbolic reminder to The United Methodist Church in North America that our brothers and sisters elsewhere in the world have kept alive this tradition of accountable discipleship. I am grateful to Dr. Kim and to the many Korean Methodists worldwide for their faithfulness and perseverance. They did not allow their church to forget its Wesleyan heritage.

There are other Methodist traditions where accountable discipleship has been kept alive through class leaders and class meetings: in the A.M.E., A.M.E. Zion, and C.M.E. Churches; in the African-American constituency of The United Methodist Church; and in a number of sister Methodist churches throughout the world. As we go back to these Wesleyan roots, we shall have much to learn from each other.

I wish to thank those who have helped to bring covenant discipleship groups to their present stage of development, and have encouraged me to explore the further possibility of revitalizing the office of class leader. My colleagues at the General Board of Discipleship continue to provide a stimulating context for these initiatives as they wrestle with God's vision of the church. No one does more in this regard than the General Secretary, Ezra Earl Jones, who has seen for many years the need to focus Christian leadership on the task which awaits us in the world rather than that which weighs us down in the church. I am grateful to Victor Pérez-Silvestry, Associate General Secretary, for his valued administrative support. And I owe a special word of thanks to my colleagues in the Office of Covenant Discipleship and Christian Formation: Phyllis Tyler-Wayman, Marigene Chamberlain, and Metral Smith. They allow me the freedom to engage in a project such as this, and provide me with a trustworthy Christian community in which to share the rough places and the plain.

At Discipleship Resources, the helpful suggestions of Craig B. Gallaway and David L. Hazlewood have greatly improved the text, and the creativity of J. Lee Bonnet is once again evident in the design of the volume. My thanks are also due to Stephen L. Potter for his keen promotion of the project, and to Connie Dillingham for her careful preparation of the manuscript.

The book is dedicated to two congregations in the Methodist tradition: Hexham Road Methodist Church in Throckley, England, where I spent my formative years as a Christian disciple; and Grace United Methodist Church in East St. Louis, Illinois, where I spent my formative years as a Christian pastor. I remain deeply indebted to each of them for guidance and nurture they may not have realized they were providing. It will surely be one of the delightful surprises at the reception for the heavenly feast to be thanked for the many blessings we have unknowingly imparted to others. The members of the Hexham Road and Grace congregations will have to stand in that receiving line for a long, long time.

General Board of Discipleship   January 1991
Nashville, Tennessee

Preface

From "Methodist Polity," by Bishop H.M. Turner, approved in 1888 by the General Conference of the African Methodist Episcopal Church, and reprinted in 1986 by the A.M.E.C. Sunday School Union.

Next to the Word of God, Methodist ministers and class leaders should familiarize themselves with the General Rules. They furnish material for the pulpit, for the class-room, for the mourner, for the backslider, for the sinner, as well as for the Christian. No one observing the provisions of these rules will ever lose membership in the church, the respect and confidence of civil society, nor a place at the right hand of God when done with earth.

Introduction
A New Generation of Leaders

VITAL CONGREGATIONS—FAITHFUL DISCIPLES

At an international "Gathering" held at Fort Worth, Texas, in the fall of 1990, The United Methodist Church was summoned by its Council of Bishops to a vision: *Vital Congregations—Faithful Disciples*. Declaring that the people of God called United Methodist have come to a critical turning point in their history, the bishops challenged them to follow Jesus Christ into a new era:

> The church is the people called to witness to God's saving action in Jesus Christ. God offers to all who will believe an infinite, redeeming love made known in the cross and in the resurrection of Jesus Christ. As the resurrection promises, God intends to transform this world into a new creation. When that times comes, God will be all in all, and people will live together in wholeness, harmony, justice, and peace. The church is the community of those who expect that new creation, and whose actions point towards its coming. "The kingdom of God has come near," Jesus announced (Mark 1:15), and so the church proclaims today through every word and deed.[1]

The bishops further declared that the only way for Christians to serve as heralds of this kingdom is to place Christ at the center of the church's life and work. Only as Christ's ministry is active through congregational mission and personal discipleship can the church see the new direction in which God is leading. Those of us called United Methodists will be vital congregations and faithful disciples only as we join with one another around the world "in proclaiming our hope in Jesus Christ, and affirming our commitment to Christ's ministry and mission today."[2]

THE LOVE AND THE JUSTICE OF GOD

In giving shape to this vision, the bishops charged the church not only to proclaim Jesus as the Christ, but also to exemplify the love and the justice of God embodied in Jesus of Nazareth. Vital congregations must equip the people of God not only to witness to Christ in everyday life, but also to practice care and hospitality; not only to be faithful in the ministries of word and sacrament, instructing people in the scriptures and fostering the disciplines of prayer and fasting, but also to join with Christ in ministries of justice, hope, and peace, obeying his commandments to feed the hungry, clothe the naked, visit the sick and those in prison, and reach out to those who are in pain, who are neglected, and who are sinned against.

If this vision is to be realized, a new generation of leaders is needed in The United Methodist Church:

> Congregations are the basic communities of faith within which new leaders for the church must be identified, called, prepared, and supported. The raising up of committed imaginative leaders is a gift of the Holy Spirit and a sign of life in Christ. For it is Christ who calls leaders for God's mission in the world, and the Spirit who gives them the gifts of leadership.[3]

RE-TRADITIONING CLASSES AND CLASS LEADERS

It is the premise of this book and its two companion volumes, *Covenant Discipleship* and *Class Leaders* (Discipleship Resources order nos. DR091B and DR092B), that the source of the new leadership called for by the bishops is to be found in the Methodist traditions of class meetings and class leaders, both of which have been long neglected and much misunderstood. The time has come to "tradition" them again: to go back to their origins, to see them in their historical context, to re-interpret them in light of the gospel, and to re-appropriate them for the ministry and mission of Jesus Christ in the world of today.

LEADERSHIP IN THE CHURCH

Part One of the book addresses the issues of leadership in the contemporary church, showing how a self-indulgent view of discipleship has displaced Christ from the center of much of our congregational life, thus depriving the church of its proper identity. The only true role for the people of God is that of a sign community—the sign of God's covenant to redeem the world in Christ. If Christ is not at the center of everything the church attempts to be and to do, then its light is hid under a bushel, its salt lacks taste, its leaven is inert, and its seed is barren.

Christ, and Christ alone, must be honored by disciples who wish to be faithful, and must be at the center of congregations that wish to be vital. The only way for this to be accomplished is for leaders in the congregation to accept responsibility for the forming of Christian disciples, and for the congregation as a whole to acknowledge and respect their leadership. This will require considerable adjustment in congregations where discipleship is viewed largely as a personal and private matter, and where leadership consists primarily of seeking to retain the maximum number of members by requiring the minimum in obligations—what Juan Luis Segundo has called "The General Rule of Pastoral Prudence."[4]

THE CONTEXT FOR LEADERSHIP

Part Two of the book describes how to introduce and develop covenant discipleship groups as the context for this leadership. Patterned after the early Methodist class meeting, these groups have become established in recent years throughout the United States and in a number of other countries around the world. Meeting for one hour each week, the members hold themselves mutually accountable to covenants they themselves write—covenants that have shaped and in turn been shaped by the General Rule of Discipleship: "To witness to Jesus Christ in the world, and to follow his teachings through acts of compassion, justice, worship, and devotion, under the guidance of the Holy Spirit."

These groups provide a context for developing leaders in discipleship, not because the members excel in their Christian living, nor yet because they have a closer relationship with Christ. They serve their congregations as role models in discipleship quite simply because they hold themselves accountable. They monitor their obedience to Jesus Christ in the company of trusted friends. They understand only too well how easy it is to slip into disobedience— or worse, to form their discipleship around their own preferences rather than the teachings of Jesus.

IMPLEMENTING LEADERSHIP

Part Three of the book deals with how to implement this leadership by recovering an office that once was the very fiber of Methodism: the class leader. Class leaders are those persons in a congregation who are willing to help with forming the discipleship of a number of other church members. In turn, class leaders are formed by covenant discipleship. This does not mean that everyone who belongs to a covenant discipleship group should be a class leader; but everyone who is a class leader should belong to a covenant discipleship group.

Recovering this tradition will require some major adjustments, not only on the part of congregations, but also on the part of pastors. Just as they share leadership with laypersons in the administrative and programmatic dimensions of the church's ministry, so pastors will have to accept shared leadership in the forming of Christian disciples. The work of James D. Anderson and Ezra Earl Jones proves timely and helpful in this regard. Distinguishing between "transactional leadership" as that which governs the institutional maintenance of the church, and "transformational leadership" as that which calls and enables the church to live out God's vision for the world, they show how both modes of leadership are necessary for vital congregations and faithful disciples. They also argue convincingly that transactional leadership has come to hold a virtual monopoly in today's congregations, robbing them of God's vision and reducing them to administrative and programmatic institutions.

NO SHORTCUTS

The recovery of the office of class leader can be an important step toward revitalizing transformational leadership, and thus restoring the necessary balance. But pastors and lay people alike must be ready to accept the hard work this will involve; for there can be no shortcuts. The call to faithful discipleship will require the fulfillment of long overdue worldly obligations, rather than yet another quest for supposedly unclaimed spiritual benefits. The call to congregational vitality will require the acceptance of down-to-earth supervision by hitherto unrecognized lay leadership, rather than yet another round of pastoral rhetoric as a way of avoiding obedience to Jesus Christ in the world. And both of these requirements are likely to occasion a marked degree of initial inconvenience.

If they manage to recover this tradition, however, United Methodists may well do more than help themselves toward faithful discipleship and congregational vitality. They may find that in this distinctive model of lay leadership they have a unique contribution to make to the world church at a critical moment in God's saving history. Such, at least, is the prayerful hope in which this book has been written.

PART ONE

Christian Formation in the Congregation

Christian disciples are formed by shaping their lives according to the General Rule of Discipleship: "To witness to Jesus Christ in the world, and to follow his teachings through acts of compassion, justice, worship, and devotion, under the guidance of the Holy Spirit." For this to happen, congregations must be wholly centered on Jesus Christ.

Chapter One

Discipleship Inside Out

THE COMING REIGN OF GOD

The center of the biblical message is a dramatic declaration of good news: God's redemption of planet earth. The imagery is rich, and the promises are specific. We are to expect a new age, a new day, a new order, when the wolf shall dwell with the lamb, the leopard shall lie down with the kid, and the lion shall eat straw like the ox; when there will be no more sound of weeping, nor cries of distress; when all children shall live beyond infancy, and all old people shall live out their days; when those who build houses shall live in them, not others; when those who plant vineyards shall eat of them, not others; when justice shall roll down like waters, and righteousness like an everflowing stream; when peoples shall beat their swords into plowshares, and their spears into pruning hooks; when nation shall not lift up sword against nation, and shall not learn war any more; when all the earth shall be as full of the knowledge of God as the waters cover the sea; and when all peoples will know who is their God, from the least of them to the greatest (Isa. 2:4; 11:6ff.; 65:20-25; Amos 5:24; Jer. 31:34).

THE PROMISES OF JESUS

The promises find supreme expression in the words of Second Isaiah, with which Jesus announced his ministry in the synagogue at Nazareth:

> The Spirit of the Lord God is upon me, because he has anointed me to bring good news to the poor. He has sent me to proclaim release to the captives and recovery of sight to the blind, to let the oppressed go free, to proclaim the year of the Lord's favor (Luke 4:18-19; Isa. 61:1-2).

Jesus talked repeatedly of the kingdom of God, the reign of God, as the time when these things would come to pass. But the dramatic significance of his announcement in the Nazareth synagogue was that God was honoring these promises that very day in the hearing of his audience. His words carried the power, not only of

1

future promise, but of a present breaking into history of the new age that would one day come to fulfillment (Luke 4:21).

It is therefore no surprise to find Jesus teaching his disciples to pray for the coming of God's kingdom, on earth as in heaven (Matt. 6:10), and to find the same hope in the early church: that in the kingdom of God there will be neither Jew nor Greek, neither slave nor free, neither male nor female, but the unity of all people in Christ (Gal. 3:28).

DEEP MYSTERIES

Yet the worldly reality of this coming reign of God makes it a difficult concept to grasp. On the one hand, it is simple and dramatic; but on the other hand, it is deeply mysterious. It is simple inasmuch as a little child can receive it, readily and spontaneously. Little children know instinctively about the signs of the kingdom of God: love, joy, kindness, and goodness. Indeed, one of the most powerful object lessons of Jesus was his presentation of a little child as exemplar of God's new humanity (Matt. 18:1-4).

Yet the kingdom of God is also mysteriously elusive, and in more ways than one. First, there is the enigma of a good and beautiful creation that has gone wrong. Planet earth retains much of its Creator's design, with bountiful blessings and continuous new life. But it is also permeated with evil and death, and warped by human sin. How and why this should have happened is a deep mystery, and quite beyond any rational explanation. The evil and suffering of the world are altogether indiscriminate, and the perversions of sin far exceed human ingenuity—as in the genocides which continue to plague the course of history.

Indeed, so bad is the disfigurement of this corner of God's creation that Jesus could only describe it as sabotage:

> The kingdom of heaven may be compared to someone who sowed good seed in his field; but while everybody was asleep, an enemy came and sowed weeds among the wheat, and then went away. So when the plants came up and bore grain, then the weeds appeared as well. And the slaves of the householder came and said to him, 'Master, did you not sow good seed in your field? Where, then, did these weeds come from?' He answered, 'An enemy has done this' (Matt. 13:24-28).

The victory against this enemy is assured. Sin, evil, and suffering will one day be purged, as Jesus made clear in the conclusion of the parable (Matt. 13:28-30). But in the meantime, there is the further mystery of a God who has dared strange things in order to redeem this wayward planet. For the Creator of the universe to appear in human form, to share in human sin and suffering, and directly to confront evil and death, was to risk a very great deal indeed. The risk has proved to be eminently worthwhile; but that does nothing at all to diminish it. Indeed, it renders the Christ event all the more awesome. What God risked and accomplished in Jesus of Nazareth has the rest of creation "waiting on tiptoe" to see the children of God revealed (Rom. 8:19).

Yet another dimension of the mystery lies in the fact that the drama is not yet ended. If the breaking in of the reign of God is beyond our comprehension, no less incomprehensible is the delay in its fulfillment. The questions are profound and legitimate: Why, with Jesus of Nazareth among us, raised from the dead and present in the power of the Holy Spirit, should sin, evil, and suffering continue? Why should the redemption of planet earth be taking so long to unfold?

HUMAN FREEDOM

One answer to these questions is to point to the freedom which God has bestowed on humankind. Not only have human beings been given the freedom to accept or reject the laws of God—a freedom which they have consistently chosen to abuse—but they have also been given the radical choice of accepting or rejecting God's redemption in Jesus Christ. This too, as even a cursory reading of human history makes clear, has been repeatedly and persistently abused. God's overtures of forgiveness and reconciliation have been spurned—even the offer made supremely from the cross.

The logic of such an argument is appealing, but it does not explain the mystery. The savagery of human beings toward one another far exceeds mere freedom of choice and the bad judgment, immaturity, and misbehavior that come with it. Besides this, the whole of planet earth has suffered and continues to suffer pain, disaster, and disease, for reasons which cannot be attributed to human sin. There is also the mystery of fate and fortune—the countless accidents of birth throughout the ages which have dealt long life and wealth to some, but short and tragic lives to millions of others.[5]

The cry of the psalmist, poignant in the days of the Old Testament, rings down the ages through Auschwitz and Vietnam and Northern Ireland and El Salvador with an anguish that is well-nigh unbearable: "How long, O Lord, how long?" (Ps. 6:3; 13:1-2; 74:10; 94:3).

GOD'S SALVATION

God's answer to this cry is as profound as the anguish out of which it is wrung: Planet earth will be saved, and will become a wholly new creation. Far from an endless perpetuation of what we presently experience, there will be a transformation of human history, in which time and eternity will be fused into a wholly new reality—an eternal life, not of immortality, but of resurrection.

God's salvation will be the ultimate triumph of love and justice and peace: the defeat of evil, the end of pain and suffering, and the dissolution of sin in all of its forms—personal, social, and systemic. God's salvation will be the final glorification of Christ as the Savior of our planet, truly acknowledged as the forerunner of a new humanity, redeemed and restored to the image of God. To use that wonderful Hebrew word, there will be *shalom*, "the peace of God, which surpasses all understanding" (Phil. 4:7).

Yet the fullness of this remains in God's mysterious future. We do not yet have universal *shalom*. We have the assurance of it in the crucial act of God's saving drama: Christ has died and Christ has risen. But the final act awaits: Christ has yet to return in glory as befits the ruler of our planet. In the meantime, he continues to minister to the world through the power of the Holy Spirit, in the same way he ministered as Jesus of Nazareth. Through his disciples, he continues to feed the hungry, clothe the naked, visit the sick and the imprisoned (Matt. 25:31-46); and he continues to identify with the outcasts of the world, content to be seen as "a glutton and a drunkard, a friend of tax collectors and sinners" (Matt. 11:19). In other words, God's plan of salvation continues to be bold and daring.

CALLED TO BE COLLEAGUES OF GOD

This is where God's mystery involves the people who call themselves Christians. It is strange indeed that God should have chosen as colleagues in these daring acts of salvation a community of people known as the church. Their part in the drama is limited, but it is critical. They have been entrusted with the singular task of letting the people of the world know what God has done and is doing to redeem their planet; and they have been gifted with the firstfruits of God's salvation in their life and work. But they are very ordinary people, these church folk, and much of the time they are barely competent for their task. It is deeply mysterious, to them and to the rest of the world, why they should have been chosen for such important work.

If Christians are to understand their role, therefore, and undertake their task with integrity, they must not evade the mysteries of God's salvation; nor must they try to resolve them. Christians must rather seek to join with the risen Christ *in the midst of* the mysteries, proclaiming the hope of the gospel. They must work faithfully in the world, waiting expectantly for God's redemption to be fulfilled, and wrestling with the tensions of a message which points to the future. To do all of this, they must be centered on Christ, empowered by the Holy Spirit; and they must be formed into faithful, obedient disciples. Nothing less will suffice.

COSTLY DISCIPLESHIP

This is why Jesus made very clear to his first followers what it would mean to become his disciples:

> Whoever comes to me and does not hate father and mother, wife and children, brothers and sisters, yes, and even life itself cannot be my disciple. Whoever does not carry the cross and follow me cannot be my disciple (Luke 14:26-27).

The invitation to follow Jesus was not to be considered lightly, or accepted thoughtlessly:

> For which of you, intending to build a tower, does not first sit down and estimate the cost, to see whether he has enough to complete it? Otherwise, when he has laid a foundation and is not able to finish, all who see it will begin to ridicule him, saying, "This fellow began to build and was not able to finish." Or what king, going out to wage war against another king, will not sit down first and consider whether he is able with ten thousand to oppose the one who comes against him with twenty thousand? If he cannot, then, while the other is still far away, he sends a delegation and asks for the terms of peace" (Luke 14:28-32).

DEVOTION AND OBEDIENCE

What is more, time and again Jesus cautioned his disciples that they would find it impossible to walk with him and hold on to worldly possessions. Their devotion to God had to be absolute: They could not divide their loyalty (Matt. 6:24). They had to be ready to surrender everything for the sake of the kingdom of God (Luke 14:33). Thus, the rich man who was invited to follow him, but was unwilling to give up his considerable possessions, was allowed to go away, shocked and grieving (Mark 10:22).

The conditions of discipleship are the same today for those who want to follow the risen Christ:

> "You shall love the Lord your God with all your heart, and with all your soul, and with all your mind." This is the greatest and first commandment. And a second is like it: "You shall love your neighbor as yourself." On these two commandments hang all the law and the prophets (Matt. 22:37-40).

Obeying these commandments is not an option for disciples of Jesus Christ. On the contrary, obedience is the *condition* of their relationship with him:

> This is my commandment, that you love one another as I have loved you. No one has greater love than this, to lay down one's life for one's friends. You are my friends if you do what I command you (John 15:12-14).

DISCIPLINED LIVING

As colleagues of the risen Christ, helping to fulfill God's plan of salvation, Christian disciples have a clear identity. They are heralds of *shalom*. They are salt, light, leaven, and seed of the coming reign of God (Matt. 5:13-14; 13:31-33). To accept this identity means a very intentional way of life; which is why "disciple" and "discipline" come from the same Latin word, *discipulus*. This is best translated today as a "special student," someone who has undertaken to study with a particular teacher in great depth, and who therefore has arranged his or her life to make such study possible. Christian disciples must expect to order their priorities in the same way, and arrange their lives so that they are "disciplined" in following the teachings of Jesus.

A MIXED TRACK RECORD

It goes without saying that in the 2,000 years since the days of the first disciples, Christians have had a very mixed track record as "disciplined" followers of Jesus Christ. Indeed, there have been times in Christian history when horrendous things have been done in the name of the teacher from Nazareth: when war has been waged in the name of the prince of peace; when death has been exacted in the name of the lord of life; when suffering has been imposed in the name of the great healer; and when the rich have sought wealth in the name of the one who identified with the poor.

Yet there have always been those who have responded to the Jewish carpenter with integrity. Not only have their spiritual gifts been much in evidence, but their faithfulness and obedience to the teachings of Jesus have provided us with important role models for Christian discipleship. And there have been times in Christian history when these persons have been in sufficient numbers to allow the Holy Spirit to move through the church with power.

EARLY METHODIST ROLE MODELS

The early Methodist revival was such a time, and it was filled with such role models. In the words of the founding leader, John Wesley, the movement had its origins toward the end of 1739, when

> eight or ten persons came to me in London . . . deeply convinced of sin, and earnestly groaning for redemption. They desired (as did two or three more the next day) that I would spend some time with them in prayer, and advise them how to flee from the wrath to come. . . . I appointed a day when they might all come together, which from thenceforward they did every week, namely, on Thursday, in the evening. . . . This was the rise of the United Society, first in London, and then in other places. Such a Society is no other than 'a company of men "having the form, and seeking the power of godliness," united in order to pray together, to receive the word of exhortation, and to watch over one another in love, that they may help each other to work out their salvation.'[6]

As their name implies, the early Methodists were noted for the *method* of their discipleship. The passage we have just cited comes from their *General Rules* of 1743, in which John Wesley laid out some guidelines for Christian living in the world, at once very straightforward and practicable. The method consisted of identifying the essential components of Christian discipleship, and then making sure they were carried out. In this way, Methodists could avoid the two cardinal errors of the Christian life: legalism and license.

COMPONENTS OF CHRISTIAN DISCIPLESHIP

Wesley grouped the components of Christian discipleship under two broad headings: "works of mercy" (doing everything possible to serve God and one's neighbor, while avoiding those things that offend God and harm one's neighbor); and "works of piety" (doing everything needful to be open to God's grace).

The works of mercy are listed in the *Rules* in some detail, and are an interesting reflection of eighteenth-century English life. They are also a rebuke to those of us in the late twentieth century who avoid making such lists (lest we be obliged to honor them). The works of piety are those time-honored disciplines of the church that open us to God's grace: public worship, the ministries of word and sacrament, private prayer, reading the Bible, and fasting or temperance. Once again, to read through the list is to be reminded how seldom these are faithfully or methodically practiced today.

WEEKLY ACCOUNTABILITY

In order to make sure that these works of mercy and piety were actually performed—and, just as important, that they were held in proper balance—the *General Rules* also stipulated a weekly meeting for all the society members, at which they were to hold themselves mutually accountable for their Christian living in the world. These weekly gatherings were known as "class meetings," and their history is described in more detail in the companion volume, *Covenant Discipleship.* Introduced initially as a method of collecting money for a building debt, they quickly became the most important feature of early Methodism. Wesley described them as the "sinews" of the movement, and there is little doubt that they were the key to the disciplined living of the members.

A number of modern-day Methodists are convinced that this straightforward method of discipleship—the disciplines of seeking God and serving neighbor, held in balance through mutual accountability—is no less practicable today. Using the early class meeting as a model, they have formed *covenant discipleship groups,* which meet for one hour each week so that the members may hold themselves mutually accountable for their discipleship. They do this by writing a covenant, in which they agree on the basics of their Christian living in the world. Then, at their weekly meetings, they go through the covenant, clause by clause, telling each other how they have fared on their Christian pilgrimage since last they were together. First formed in 1975, covenant discipleship groups now function throughout the United States and in a number of other countries around the world.

THE GENERAL RULE OF DISCIPLESHIP

In adopting the early class meeting as their model, covenant discipleship groups have not copied the early class meeting. Rather, they have "traditioned" it—that is, they have taken the essence of the class meeting as it functioned in early Methodism, and appropriated it for today in light of the gospel. In so doing, they have also traditioned the *General Rules*. Taking the essentials of the *Rules*—"works of mercy" and "works of piety"—and appropriating them for the church of today, covenant discipleship groups have formulated a *General Rule of Discipleship:*

> *To witness to Jesus Christ in the world,*
> *and to follow his teachings through*
> *acts of compassion, justice, worship, and devotion,*
> *under the guidance of the Holy Spirit.*

To witness to Jesus Christ means not only proclaiming him as prophet and redeemer, but also calling on all people to acknowledge him as sovereign of the coming reign of God. It means not only obeying the teachings of Jesus, but also making clear whose teachings they are. Jesus left his disciples in no doubt at all that he expected this testimony from them (Luke 9:26).

Acts of compassion are those simple, basic things we do out of kindness to our neighbor; and our neighbor is anyone who is in need, anywhere in the world. To the extent that we feed the hungry, clothe the naked, and visit the sick and the imprisoned, we minister to Christ in our midst.

Acts of justice remind us that God thundered the law from Sinai and pronounced righteousness through the prophets. We must not only minister to people in need, but ask why they are in need in the first place. And if they are being treated unjustly, then we must confront the persons or systems that cause the injustice.

Acts of worship are the means of grace that we exercise corporately: the ministries of word and sacrament. Not only do they affirm the indispensable place of the church in Christian discipleship. They also enable us to build each other up in the Body of Christ.

Acts of devotion are those private spiritual disciplines of prayer, reading the scriptures, and inward examination, that bring us face to face with God most directly, when no one else is present. At such times, our dialogue with God is intensely personal, searching, and enriching.

The General Rule concludes with an affirmation that discipleship is not only a lifestyle, but also a relationship. Figure 1 shows that, along with the "form" of discipleship (the teachings of Jesus) there must be the "power" (the presence of the Holy Spirit in our lives). In this way, we are more likely to avoid the errors of legalism and license. Failure to heed the teachings of Jesus can quickly lead to irresponsible behavior rather than spiritual freedom. But by the same token, the teachings of Jesus quickly become a legalistic impossibility without the grace and power of the Holy Spirit.

MERCY

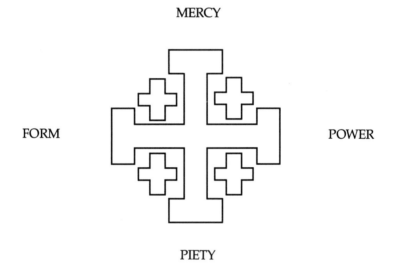

FORM   POWER

PIETY

FIGURE 1: THE FORM AND POWER OF DISCIPLESHIP

As Figure 2 further makes clear, the four-fold method of the General Rule is wholly interactive. When it is practiced with accountability, all the dimensions of discipleship are interdependent. Concerns for social justice are honed and steeped in vigils of prayer; deepened knowledge of the scriptures impels us to servanthood in the world; the God who is Spirit is worshiped as the God whose justice favors the widow and the orphan; and the God who calls to ever-deepening communion is recognized as the God whose prophets denounced the inequities of rich and poor.

By seeking to follow this General Rule, Christians are regularly confronted, not by the false God-question, "Do you believe in God?" but rather by the true God-question, *"In which God do you believe?*". By practicing the disciplines of the Rule regularly and methodically, disciples open themselves to the Holy Spirit as faithful channels of grace for service in the world. Corporately, they become the vital congregations that are sign communities of the coming reign of God.

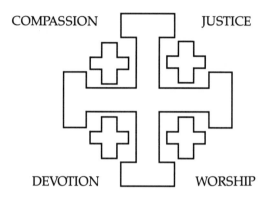

COMPASSION   JUSTICE

DEVOTION   WORSHIP

FIGURE 2: THE GENERAL RULE OF DISCIPLESHIP

A SERIOUS ANOMALY

If this General Rule is indeed a sound basis for Christian discipleship, then it immediately exposes a serious anomaly in the North American church; for this is not how the great majority of Christians in the United States live out their discipleship. The fact of the matter is that there is widespread religious belief in the United States, but much less religious practice.

Those who gather information on such matters have long been providing us with sobering statistics. In 1985 the Gallup Report published a survey, *Religion in America: 50 Years: 1935-1985*, which revealed some remarkably consistent patterns. For example, in the past five decades, 95 percent of Americans have said they believe in God or a universal spirit, and 70 percent have said they believe in the divinity of Jesus Christ; yet in the same period, only 15 percent have claimed to follow daily disciplines of prayer and Bible reading. Two-thirds of the population have maintained membership in Christian denominations; yet only one-third have been in church on any given Sunday—and for some denominations, the attendance has been much lower.[7]

Perhaps most tellingly, a survey taken in 1984 revealed that only 10 percent of the Christian population regarded their spiritual commitment as having any significant impact on their lifestyle. When asked whether they could identify with statements such as, "I try hard to put my religious beliefs into practice in my relations with all people, including people of different races, religious attitudes, and backgrounds," or "I sometimes do things I want very much NOT to do because I believe it is the will of God," 90 percent of the responses were negative.[8]

LOW EXPECTATIONS

Anyone who is involved to a measurable degree with the life and work of the North American church will hardly be surprised by these statistics. Those of us who have leadership responsibilities, whether we are clergy or laity, know only too well how difficult it is to generate support and attendance for what ought to be basic congregational activities. Worship has to be conducive to even the mildest level of interest and participation. Bible study has to have special promotion and outstanding resources. Prayer groups have to be sustained by spiritual retreats and motivational leadership. Community outreach is in the hands of a few volunteers who must learn to be persuasive and understanding in asking for help. And social justice has to be advocated in such a way as not to offend the multiplicity of viewpoints which invariably seem to be more important than singleness of action.

In short, church membership in North America does not manifest anything like the commitment Jesus called for in the New Testament, not least because our church leadership does not appear to require it. By and large, new members are presented, not with the cost of Christian discipleship, but with the benefits—a direct inversion of the invitation which appears in the New Testament.

HIGH EXPECTATIONS

As we have already noted, Jesus made clear to his earliest followers that there would be rich rewards for those who became his disciples. But he also made clear that rewards should not be the motivation for joining him. The task of discipleship was too great and the lifestyle too demanding for any who were not ready to accept hardships and frustrations along with pleasures and satisfactions. In spite of this clear warning, many of Jesus' first disciples found his teachings difficult to accept, and "no longer went about with him" (John 6:66). And when it came to the ultimate test, those closest to him failed dismally. One even betrayed him.

Yet these scriptural injunctions are rarely, if ever, explained to people who join the church today. Still less do we point out the warnings of Jesus not to take such a step lightly. It would seriously disrupt a contemporary worship service if new members were introduced as those who had most recently declared themselves ready to "hate father and mother, wife and children, brothers and sisters, yes, and even life itself" for the sake of following Jesus of Nazareth (Luke 14:26). On the contrary, new members are welcomed into communities of supportive love, and urged to take advantage of plentiful programs. To the extent that they are presented with the demands of Christian discipleship at all, the conditions are usually limited to basic doctrinal beliefs, which may or may not be preceded or accompanied by instruction in the faith.

This tends to be the pattern, irrespective of theological persuasion. It can happen in liberal and conservative congregations, and everything in between. The church that gives priority to the "born again" experience and the one that focuses on "human development" are both susceptible to the error of offering Christian benefits to the detriment or even the denial of Christian obligations. On the one hand, the Christian life can be presented as the pursuit of spiritual enrichment while neglecting the more routine and less dramatic ways in which Christian discipleship is properly nurtured. On the other hand, what ought to be a spiritual quest can be presented as an exercise in self-fulfillment, spurning the critical dynamic of Christian discipleship—obedience to Jesus Christ. In both instances, Christian formation is misunderstood, or neglected altogether.

CHURCHLY PREOCCUPATIONS

There are two reasons for this dearth of Christian formation in our congregational life. The first is practical, and the second theological. The practical reason is that much of our present North American church leadership is consumed with membership enrollment. Indeed, the concern has grown dangerously close to idolatry. Where there is increase in membership, the growth is often viewed as success, with little heed for the ways in which the new members can further the coming reign of God. Where there is decline, all too often the concern is how this affects the church rather than the extent to which it handicaps the work of Jesus Christ in the world.

The idolatry in all of this lies in the preoccupation of the church with its own health and image—a contradiction in terms we shall examine in more detail in Chapter 2. The consequence in practical terms is that the conditions of Christian discipleship are frequently compromised in order to attract more people into membership. Likewise the cost of Christian discipleship is frequently minimized lest it prove an obstacle to existing members, many of whom have been attracted to the church in the hope of finding the sense of community which a competitive and individualistic culture does not provide. It is hardly surprising that the scriptural language of discipleship is deemed inappropriate for such churchly distractions.

PERSONALIZED SALVATION

The theological issue is at once more subtle and profound. It concerns the personalizing of God's salvation; and ironically, it stems from one of the great riches of the Protestant Reformation: the doctrine of justification.[9]

As stated by the early Protestant reformers, the significance of this doctrine is its radical freedom: the freedom of the individual believer to be forgiven and reconciled with God through Jesus Christ, with no other intermediary. It proclaims to each and every person that salvation is by grace alone, and that the only condition of this gracious salvation is to receive it by faith. It assures each sinner of the supreme privilege of standing before God, acceptable again as part of the divine family. Through the merits of Jesus Christ, our relationship with God is restored, and the Holy Spirit enters into our lives with grace and power.

Along with these blessings, however, comes a hidden danger; and it lies in the assurance with which the Holy Spirit confirms our restored relationship to God. If the great freedom of "justification by grace through faith" is that each believer has a personal relationship with God through Christ, the great pitfall of the doctrine is that the experience of this new relationship can assume an exaggerated importance in the life of the believer. Put differently, attaining and sustaining a personal assurance of salvation can distract from the purpose of Christian discipleship, which is to join with Jesus Christ in the unfinished task of God's salvation. True faith in Christ brings obligations as well as benefits.

PRIVILEGE WITH A PURPOSE

The key to Christian discipleship is an awareness that our new relationship with God in Christ is a privilege with a purpose. The privilege is that in the midst of God's mysterious redemption, described by Paul as the groaning of creation in labor pains (Rom. 8:22), Christians are allowed a foretaste of *shalom*. We are baptized by the Holy Spirit, and we experience the firstfruits of eternal life here and now—the peace of God that passes all understanding. But just as Jesus was anointed by the Holy Spirit *in order to* carry out his ministry (Luke 4:18-19), so we too receive the baptism of the Holy Spirit *in order to* proclaim the coming reign of God, and embody it with living hope and anticipation.

THE PITFALL OF FAITH

Understanding the purpose of this privilege is one of the most important insights of the Christian life, and it does not come easily. Indeed, from the very beginning of the church, delight in the firstfruits of *shalom* rather than application to the task of preparing for its fulfillment has been a pitfall for Christian disciples. We can see this in the Epistle of James, which cautions against a faith that does not lead to good works. Some New Testament scholars suggest that this letter, coming later than the Pauline epistles, was written because Paul's teaching on grace, aimed in large measure against the legalism of the Jews, was being misinterpreted by the early church as a denial of the law altogether—something which, as Jesus himself made clear, was not at all the intent of the gospel (Matt. 5:17-20). Grace does not deny the law of God, but rather fulfills it.

Given the central tenet of justification by faith, however, it is no coincidence that Martin Luther, one of the doctrine's chief architects, should have described James as "an epistle of straw." As far as Luther was concerned, the heart of the gospel was grace for each believer, received by faith alone, for which the sole authority was scripture. At a time when the church imposed all sorts of priestly conditions on its members, this was a trumpet blast of freedom. But as the compass-heading of a major new tradition of the church, it has proved to be a course-correction which itself requires considerable correction. "Justification by grace through faith" has often been interpreted as "justification by faith," a misunderstanding which has placed such an emphasis on faith that the common sense of Christian living in the world, accumulated through centuries of tradition, has often been rashly disregarded.

When this has happened, Christian discipleship has become much more a matter of right belief than right action, right perspective rather than right concern, and right experience rather than right involvement. And since the Reformation took place at a time when printing had become widely available, the various traditions of Protestantism have found it all the more difficult to avoid the mistake of making the gospel more "word" than "deed"—what Frederick Herzog has perceptively termed "God-talk" as opposed to "God-walk."[10]

THE METHODIST EXCEPTION

The major exception to this pitfall in the history of Protestantism has been the Methodist tradition, and in particular the writings of John Wesley. Wesley was steeped in the doctrines of the Church of England, whose sixteenth-century theologians had serious reservations about Luther's teaching on justification. They understood the theological depth and richness of the doctrine; but they also understood that ordinary people need practical guidelines for daily living in the world. In their view, a doctrine which gave everyone the freedom to take one's cue directly from God seemed to be fraught with ambivalence and mischief.

Accordingly, the doctrine and discipline drawn up by the early Church of England gave emphasis to works no less than faith in the Christian life. The grace of God in Christ was still at the center of the message of salvation; but good works were an appropriate response to grace no less than faith. In contrast to Lutheran teaching, the Epistle of James figured prominently in the doctrinal *Homilies* of 1543, which Wesley edited and published early in his ministry. The message in these homilies was nothing if not clear: Faith without works is dead and devilish.[11]

THE "METHOD" OF METHODISM

As traditioned by John Wesley, this became the doctrinal basis for the "method" of Methodism. It caused a great deal of controversy throughout his life, but his position was consistent: Salvation is a gift from God, accomplished for us by Christ and Christ alone; the condition of this salvation is faith and faith alone; but in turn, the sole condition of faith is obedience to the teachings of Jesus Christ. Thus, while good works are not necessary to earn our salvation, they are necessary to *keep* it.

Unfortunately, Methodists have by and large failed to hold to this "method" of discipleship; though there are some encouraging signs that those of us in North America might now be giving it some reconsideration. There is a renewed interest in the Wesleyan heritage, fostered in large measure by the commitment of The United Methodist Publishing House to a new and definitive edition of Wesley's *Works;* and there is more frequent dialogue with Methodist traditions in the Third World, where rules for Christian living are seen to be by no means incompatible with faithful discipleship.

All of this is beginning to impact the ministry and mission of United Methodist congregations. In the meantime, however, the popular view of discipleship still tends to be that of right belief rather than right action. And when this is played out in the context of an individualistic, consumer-oriented culture such as late twentieth-century North America, the results are little short of disastrous for the coming reign of God. In our concern to maximize the benefits of the Christian life and minimize the obligations, we deny center stage to Jesus Christ, lest he should challenge our priorities and perceptions, or subvert our carefully structured goals, objectives, and strategies. In other words, our prevailing view of discipleship costs us our Christian integrity, and even our Christian identity.

SCRIPTURAL DISCOMFORTS

Needless to say, the contrast between the average pattern of churchly activity in North America and the sharp, abrasive conditions of discipleship laid down by Jesus causes us considerable discomfort. It is one thing to accept God's forgiveness and reconciliation in Christ, and then do one's best to live out that salvation according to the commandments of God. It is quite another to be ready to abandon job and home and family for the sake of Jesus Christ, and to accept ridicule, persecution, or even death, for the sake of the kingdom of God. As we have noted, conditions such as these are not requirements for church membership in the average North American congregation; nor do we present them as live options for faithful Christian living. Must the call of Jesus to discipleship therefore remain impossibly radical—consigned to pulpit or Sunday school class or Bible study as an ideal which is always worth considering, but not really within our reach?

From the perspective of our Protestant pitfall, the answer to this question is bound to lack enthusiasm. For one thing, when faith in Christ is the priority of our discipleship, we ourselves are the focus of attention. We tend to measure our capacity for serving Christ by what *we* consider to be our gifts and graces; and the criterion of these self-assessments will tend to be that of personal preference adjusted to our level of comfort. For another thing, even when we do recognize the need to revitalize our tradition of "methodical" discipleship, we are unclear as to how to proceed. The commitments of our congregations seem to be so casual and so diffuse that we despair of ever forming faithful disciples of Jesus Christ. We search for ways to invert the self-centeredness of our congregational life, but we always seem to search in vain.

CONGREGATIONAL CONTRADICTIONS

There have been times when many of us have fantasized a "night of the long knives," pruning our rolls, getting rid of the "deadwood," and honing our congregations to the level of discipleship that Jesus "really expects." Yet we know this is unrealistic; and besides, it goes against our better judgment. It is certainly not how we behave toward the typical Sunday morning congregation. The fact of the matter is, we are *glad* they are at worship. We are heartened to see them. We don't even think of turning them away, and we don't wish to deprive them of the blessings of the gospel.

Yet there is no denying our deep unease nonetheless. By accepting all persons just as they are, are we not denying what Jesus said about discipleship? Should we not send more "rich young" people away "grieving" because of their "many possessions" rather than welcome them because of their potential contributions to our budgets? Should we not be more exacting in our examination of new members, making more certain that they have indeed accepted salvation in Christ Jesus and that they do indeed have the indwell-

ing Holy Spirit, rather than adjusting our membership requirements to what we perceive to be their comfort level and orienting
our programs to what we perceive to be their needs?

DISCIPLESHIP "OUTSIDE IN"

It is at this point that we begin to see the consequences of a
discipleship that is faith-centered rather than Christ-centered.
Being a disciple requires a commitment to Jesus of Nazareth that
embodies our faith in him. Faith is merely the *means* of our commitment, not the commitment itself. If we begin to focus on our faith
in Christ to the neglect of Jesus of Nazareth and his teachings, we
adopt an "outside in" view of discipleship. The awesome salvation
proclaimed and accomplished for us by Jesus Christ is thence
reduced to the small and relatively insignificant part of it that
concerns each individual believer.

This is not to suggest that you and I as individuals are unimportant in God's plan of salvation. But we are not *that* important. God
has countless children to be brought home, and a planet to be
redeemed in every dimension of its existence; and we are commissioned to be Christ's colleagues in this task. But if we focus on our
response to God's salvation in Christ rather than on Christ himself,
we inevitably turn our attention away from these obligations and
slide toward the pitfall of self-centeredness and self-gratification.

THE ONE TRUE CENTER

The only true center of our discipleship is Jesus of Nazareth,
crucified, risen, and soon to come again. When we are centered on
Christ, we see that our salvation is truly God's gift, graciously
offered, and with no conditions other than a willingness to accept
it. It is then that we see that our new relationship with God is not
our doing—that our salvation lies in what Christ has done for us.
When we turn to God "with hearty repentance and true faith," and
when we "intend to lead a new life, following the commandments
of God, and walking from henceforth in his holy ways,"[12] we cease
to be concerned about ourselves. We become much more concerned about the God "who reconciled us to himself through
Christ" (2 Cor. 5:18).

When we are centered on Christ, we also become aware that the
salvation promised by God far exceeds any one person's acceptance
of it, or any church's understanding of it. Our salvation is not only
personal redemption. It is joining and participating in God's salva-

tion of planet earth, accomplished in Jesus Christ, and soon to be fulfilled in universal *shalom*. This glorious hope is far more certain, and far more worthy of our commitment, than anything we might experience in our own lives. The assurance of salvation does not lie in our own redemption, but in knowing we are part of God's redemption of the world.

God's salvation is indeed awesome. It is nothing less than the gathering of all created life, past, present, and future, into a new age, a new order, a new heaven, and a new earth:

> And I heard a loud voice from the throne saying,
> "See, the home of God is among mortals.
> He will dwell with them as their God;
> they will be his peoples,
> and God himself will be with them;
> he will wipe every tear from their eyes.
> Death will be no more;
> mourning and crying and pain will be no more,
> for the first things have passed away."
> (Rev. 21:3-4)

DISCIPLESHIP "INSIDE OUT"

When we view salvation from Christ's standpoint instead of our own, our discipleship becomes "inside out" rather than "outside in." We see that the true intent of his incarnation was to reach out to a *world* that God deeply loved (John 3:16). This is the bedrock of the gospel, and the purpose of our calling. For in Christ Jesus, not only was God "reconciling the world to himself, not counting their trespasses against them," but was also "entrusting the message of reconciliation to us" (2 Cor. 5:19).

This is the reason we feel the way we do about our congregations, and why we continue to give them so much of our time and energy. This is why, Sunday by Sunday, we are glad to see everyone at church, never mind how they respond to the gospel, or how they make their commitment to Christian discipleship, or how they take part in our activities. Our hearts go out to them, and we welcome them into the family of God—because that is the nature of the gospel the Holy Spirit impels us to announce and live out in the world.

CONCERN FOR THE WORLD

This is what Jesus told us to do; and more, he showed us how to do it. He reached out to people, graciously and unconditionally. When people were sick, he healed them (Matt. 9:2-8; 15:29-31; Mark 1:29-34; 2:1-12; Luke 14:1-6), even when they forgot to say thank you (Luke 17:11-19). He spoke in parables that ordinary folk could understand (Matt. 13:34-35; Mark 4:33-34). He celebrated at their weddings (John 2:1-11) and he played with their children (Mark 10:13-16). When they were stranded in the desert without food, he fed them (John 6:1-14); and always he had compassion on them (Matt. 15:32; Mark 8:2).

As his present-day disciples, we can do no less. God's people still must be fed and healed and taught and loved, and we must join with Jesus as he continues this ministry and mission to the world. In a well-churched culture such as North America, much of this feeding and healing and teaching and loving of God's people takes place in our congregations. This is why we should always be generous with the blessings we enjoy in our congregations: hearing the parables of Jesus, joining in the family community of God, being fed by the Word and the sacrament, and being healed by the grace of God. We should never discourage people from experiencing all of this: Jesus didn't discourage them.

A WIDE RANGE OF RESPONSE

Even so, the question remains: How do we connect these gracious ministries of Jesus with his blunt, if not brutal, words about discipleship? We badly need some clarification at this point.

The answer lies in the simple but radical inversion of priorities that we have just proposed. Once we have turned our discipleship inside out and focused all of our attention on Christ and Christ alone, we find an infinitely rich and varied response to his call, in ourselves and in others. Once Christ and Christ alone is the arbiter of what constitutes faithful discipleship, we find the range of Christian disciples to be virtually without limit: from those who make the most radical and costly commitments to those whose level of interest is casual at most. And if Jesus himself is willing to accept these variations, who are we to object?

The most damaging consequence of our Protestant pitfall is that we who call ourselves his disciples have usurped the role of Christ in these matters. *We* have determined what is appropriate discipleship, and have presumed to judge who meets our criteria of personal faith. Instead of witnessing to Jesus Christ and the fullness of his salvation, we have witnessed to that small part of his salvation *we* have been privileged to receive. Instead of presenting the teachings of Jesus, and allowing people to follow them with whatever grace they receive from the Holy Spirit, we have presented *our* understanding of his teachings—an understanding, let it be said again, of very limited capacity—and tried to persuade people to see things our way.

The result is that we have established a norm for Christian discipleship that not only falls far short of the teachings of Jesus, but that is also out of touch with the rest of the world, where Jesus desperately needs help with his continuing work of salvation. Instead of serving as salt and light and leaven and seed as Jesus commissioned us to serve, we have created congregational "safe houses," offering the benefits of salvation, but doing little to further God's salvation of planet earth.

The task is clear, and urgent. Not only does our discipleship need to be turned inside out. So do our congregations.

Chapter Two

Congregations Inside Out

THE TEMPORARY NATURE OF THE CHURCH

The fullness of the reign of God means the end of the church as we know it. When Christ's promises are fulfilled, no longer shall people "teach one another, or say to each other, 'Know the Lord,' for they shall all know me, from the least of them to the greatest, says the Lord" (Jer. 31:34). On that day, the work of the church will be done. There will be no more need of Christians.

This is a profound gospel truth, and it ought to be the bedrock of our Christian identity. Yet we rarely think of the church in this way; and when the truth is stated in as many words, it tends to catch us unawares. If we were truly committed to the ministry of Jesus Christ, we would realize that our task as Christians gives us a very temporary identity indeed. We are entrusted with announcing to the world the hope of God's ultimate victory in Jesus Christ. It stands to reason, therefore, that when God's victory is accomplished, it will no longer require announcing. On that day, the glory will be Christ's alone. We will share *in* it, but our role in preparing for it will be concluded.

When God's victory comes, we will be caught up into something infinitely more glorious than the church, and given an identity infinitely more gratifying than that of Christian. We will be part of a new creation: a new heaven, a new earth, a new humanity, a new order, in which our task as messengers and forerunners will be acknowledged, but redundant. We will no longer be sampling the foretaste of eternal life we presently enjoy in the church, for the heavenly feast will have begun in earnest.

THE CHURCH AS SIGN COMMUNITY

There are many theologians who have attempted to find an image for the church which projects this identity with clarity and integrity, but none has done better than the Uruguayan Jesuit, Juan Luis Segundo. Drawing on the work of Karl Rahner, but employing a theological method of praxis—i.e., allowing the teachings of Jesus to be interpreted by the discipleship of ordinary folk— Segundo identifies the church as the *sign community of the coming reign of God*.[13] Pending the fullness of God's salvation, the task of the church, and of the Christian disciples who make up its work force, is to direct the world toward the kingdom which Jesus announced and inaugurated.

To be this sign community means accepting that the mission of the church is in reality the mission of God, the work of the risen Christ and the Holy Spirit in the world. God's mission is nothing less than the gathering of the human family back home where they belong—home with God, now and for all eternity. The mission began with the call to Abraham, Moses, and the prophets. It came to full expression in the life, death, and resurrection of Jesus of Nazareth, who extended God's forgiveness and reconciliation to the world, supremely from the cross. It has continued in and through the work of the Holy Spirit, who invites all of humanity to accept God's gracious parenthood. And it will come to fulfillment with the kingdom of God on earth as in heaven: a universal reign of love and justice and peace.

If congregations are to be the sign communities Christ intended them to be, they must be subsumed by this hope and this vision. They must be so centered on the mission of God that those who belong to their company will be impelled into the world as messengers of God, servants of Jesus Christ, and channels of grace for the Holy Spirit.

SALT AND LIGHT TO THE WORLD

Jesus expressed this identity for the church in two vivid images. On the one hand, he said that Christians are to be the salt of the earth (Matt. 5:13). This is a reference to the Hebrew Bible where, in addition to being essential for life and nourishment, salt is the sign of a covenant with God (Lev. 2:13; Num. 18:19; 2 Chr. 13:5). To this day in parts of the Middle East, eating salt with someone signifies the strong mutual bonds of a covenant relationship. Salt is a substantial token of good faith.

Disciples of Jesus are thus the sign of God's new covenant with humankind, mediated by Jesus himself, that will bring the people of God into an intimate communion with their creator. They will have God's laws placed in their minds and written on their hearts (Heb. 8:10). The signature of this covenant is the church, the salt of the world. All the more reason, therefore, for Christians to be faithful. To exchange salt that is no longer salty is a token of bad faith (Mark 9:50).[14]

Another image used by Jesus is that of light. Christians are not to put their lamp under the bushel basket, but on the lampstand, where it can give light to all the house. We are to let our light shine before others, so that they may see our good works and give glory to our Father in heaven. We are to be clear and visible, like a city on a hill, since a sign by definition points to something *sign*ificant (Matt. 5:14-16).

THE PITFALL OF SELF-PREOCCUPATION

In these very qualities of good faith, visibility, and significance, however, there is a pitfall very similar to that of a self-centered discipleship. A sign can be so prominent that it ends up drawing attention only to itself. Instead of directing people to a place, or announcing an event, or issuing a warning, a sign can so impress people by its design, its coloring, or its technique that its message loses significance—as in an over-produced television commercial.

Just as Christian disciples must beware of the pitfall of a self-centered discipleship, so the church must beware of the pitfall of self-preoccupation in its task as sign community. In the same way that disciples can delight in the benefits of God's grace to the neglect of serving Jesus Christ in the world, so the church can delight in the benefits of Christian communion and fellowship to the neglect of pointing to the coming reign of God. A sign which draws attention only to itself is self-defeating.

To be faithful to its commission, the church must consistently and unequivocally point beyond itself to the reality of the coming reign of God. Self-preoccupation is the deadliest of churchly diseases.

THE CHURCH AS SUBSTITUTE COMMUNITY

One way in which the church can stumble into self-preoccupation is through the impulse to provide what is lacking in society at large. Most especially is this the case in an individualistic culture such as present-day North America, where a range of personal and social needs is not being met due to the weakening of community and family life. Starved of these basic needs, people will often gravitate toward the church simply because this is where they find a sense of belonging.

The impulse to provide this ministry is of course charitable and

Christ-like. Every congregation should be ready to care for people in need. The pitfall lies in making this the *central* focus of Christian ministry and mission. For when the church finds itself merely substituting for the deficiencies of contemporary society, it runs the risk of having its agenda set by the world; and this is by no means the same as serving Jesus Christ in the world.

MISUSING SPIRITUAL BENEFITS

Another way to the pitfall of self-preoccupation is the misuse of spiritual gifts. This is more subtle than that of being a substitute community, and therefore more deceptive. For even when congregations open themselves to the grace of God through ministry which truly embodies the firstfruits of the kingdom of God—the spiritual gifts of love, joy, peace, patience, kindness, generosity, faithfulness, gentleness, and self-control (Gal. 5:22)—even then they can be distracted from their task. Instead of regarding the spiritual blessings of Christian community as a source of strength and hope to be shared with the world, congregations can mistakenly regard them as benefits of belonging to the church—benefits which, albeit spiritual, will then tend to be used as a means of congregational self-maintenance and even self-indulgence.

Instead of places where people come to be formed as Christian disciples, congregations then become places where people are primarily concerned with being helped and blessed. Instead of finding how they can serve the risen Christ in the world, proclaiming and living out the coming reign of God, they begin to look for ways in which they themselves can be enriched by God's love and peace and justice. And even when they do make a serious attempt to form their members into Christian disciples, they will tend to focus on the development of personal spiritual growth to the neglect of helping Jesus Christ with the unfinished task of preparing the world for God's coming *shalom*.

ENCULTURATION

The most damaging effect of this pitfall is "enculturation"—the co-option of the church by the very influences it ought to be challenging through its ministry and mission. Instead of presenting the world with the gospel, the church adjusts the gospel to whatever the world finds important. This leaves the Christian community with an identity which is not a sign of the coming reign of God, but merely a reflection of what is happening in its worldly context. The false gods or idols that are always prevalent in a culture are thus readily incorporated into the church, which by contrast ought to be the living embodiment of Jesus Christ.

CULTURAL IDOLS

The noted missiologist, Charles Taber, has identified five such idols in our day and age. To emphasize that none of them is new, he has given them classical names. They are Eros, the god of unrestrained sexual expression; Dionysus, the god of self-indulgence and excess; Mammon, the divine personification of wealth; Titan, the god of autonomous human achievement in an age of technology; and Mars, the god of race and land and nation, who sets people against people in mutual hate, fear, and aggression.[15] That these can seduce Christians into adjusting the gospel to cultural values is danger enough. But even more dangerous is when the church goes further, and gives honor and blessing to some of these idols—the very things that God has repeatedly called on faithful Christians to abandon. They are rightly identified as idols, because they tear at our deepest loyalties, and arouse our deepest feelings.

A DRAIN ON RESOURCES

Quite apart from the effects of enculturation, the pitfall of self-preoccupation proves to be a devastating drain on a congregation's energies and resources. When the church sees itself primarily as a source of benefits for its members rather than a support base for serving Jesus Christ in the world, not only does it misunderstand its role as sign community of the coming reign of God. It also finds itself in a vicious circle of providing services it was never meant to provide, and for which its resources are altogether inadequate and inappropriate. Those members who are most vocal and aggressive with their needs will consume most of the energies of a church that sees itself in this light, and certainly most of the energies of their leadership.

Moreover, congregations such as these will ultimately be judged by whether these "needy" people feel their needs are being met. The integrity of their ministry will be measured, not by their faithfulness to the gospel, nor yet by their honoring of God, but rather by how many people have been satisfied by their services.

THE GENERAL RULE OF PASTORAL PRUDENCE

In one of his most influential volumes, *The Hidden Motives of Pastoral Action*, Juan Luis Segundo addresses this pitfall of the church. His analysis is cogent and persuasive. Once the church surrenders to its cultural context, he explains, it must make repeated adjustments in order to survive. In the case of the Roman Catholic Church in Latin America, this has resulted in what he calls the *General Rule of Pastoral Prudence:* "The absolute minimum in obligations in order to keep the maximum number of people."[16] And once this rule is adopted, needless to say, it becomes pastorally imprudent to add any obligations to church membership which might alienate potential new members.

As we observed in the previous chapter, Segundo's findings are by no means unfamiliar to Protestants in North America, where the church is still a major social institution. Instead of vital congregations comprising faithful disciples who seek to follow Jesus Christ intentionally and consistently, by and large we have an enculturated church seeking to offer benefits to its members—what might be described as a collection of congregational "safe houses."

THE CHURCH "SAFE HOUSE"

The reason for describing them as "safe houses" is that an enculturated church has no other identity to distinguish it from its cultural context. As Figure 3 illustrates, the enculturated congregation has to draw a clear line between itself and the rest of the world precisely because it reflects so much of the world. Its only recourse is to see itself as a place where the best of worldly values can be found—only more abundantly. This stance will often require it to reach out into the community; but from the safe house perspective, the purpose of this outreach is almost always to invite friends, neighbors, and others to share the blessings its members already enjoy.

The identity of safe house congregations lies in viewing their discipleship and their community life as sources of maximum personal benefit—a perspective that increasingly leads to alienation from those who do not share these blessings with them. To the extent that this identity shapes their day-to-day relationships, they see themselves as different from everyone else, and out of place in a world where they do not belong.

FIGURE 3: THE CHURCH "SAFE HOUSE"

CHRISTIANS IN THE WORLD

It must quickly be said that there is a very real sense in which Christians are not "of the world" (John 15:18-19; 17:16). Yet Jesus did not call on his disciples to reject the world. His mission was rather to supplant the present world order. Thus, while he declared that his kingdom was not "from this world" (John 18:36), he also sent his disciples to be "salt *of* the earth" and "light *of* the world" (Matt. 5:13-14). As his followers, Christians are to affirm the world—not the world as it is, but the world as it *will be*. Paul made the same point when he charged the Christians at Rome not to be "conformed" to this world, but to be "transformed" by the renewing of their minds (Rom. 12:2).

The purpose and the privilege of being Christian disciples, therefore, is not to be taken out of the world, nor yet to withdraw from the world, but to be part of the world in the most profound and meaningful way possible: to be citizens of the *new* earth, the *new* age, the *new* order.[17] The task of the church as the community of Christians, the Body of Christ, is to signify to the world that God is giving new birth to planet earth. The struggles we experience in the meantime are the most hopeful struggles of all—the birth pangs of a new creation (Rom. 8:22).

THE SAFE HOUSE THRESHOLD

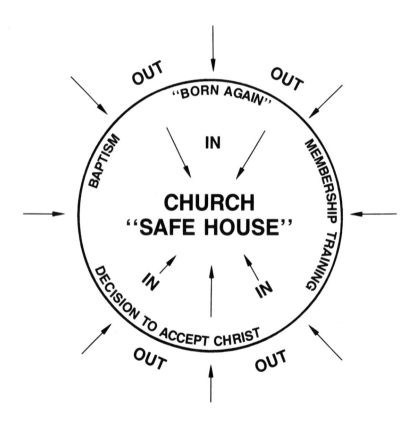

FIGURE 4: CROSSING SAFE HOUSE THRESHOLDS

A further problem with the line which separates the church safe house from the rest of the world is the question of how to get people across it. The problem is not always apparent, because in many instances the threshold is not at all explicit. Congregations competing for new members will rarely stand on ceremony when it comes to recruitment. But the church safe house by definition will always have a threshold, and new members are bound to discover it sooner or later.

The nature of the threshold will vary, depending on the tradition of a congregation or the perspective of its pastoral leadership; and so will the method of crossing it. Moreover, as illustrated in Figure 4, many of these thresholds are right and proper steps for new members to take when they join the church of Jesus Christ. The problem lies in making these steps a dividing line from the world. When a person is baptized, or born again, or accepts Christ as Savior and Lord, or goes through membership training, the purpose ought not to be a process of separation *from* the world, but a joining with Jesus Christ *in* the world—more consciously, more resolutely, and more faithfully. For that is where Jesus Christ is most readily to be found, ministering to the little ones who need him.

MINISTRIES OF ASSIMILATION

Yet another problem with the church safe house is that when people have crossed the threshold, and are "in" as opposed to "out," there is still the task of making them part of the "safe house" in a meaningful way. The strategy then becomes one of assimilation: how to make people feel that they "belong." Figure 5 shows some of the ways in which this can be done: directly, by ministering to them through nurturing and caring; or indirectly, by involving them in ministries of service. All of these are important dimensions of the life and work of a congregation, and many of them reach out into the community on behalf of the church.

If the purpose of these ministries is primarily to assimilate members, however, they will ultimately lack an overall focus and direction. There will be no center to the congregation other than the needs of its members; and this, as we have noted, inexorably leads to the pitfall of self-preoccupation. For when ministries of the church are viewed in this way, they are but a hair's breadth from becoming a self-serving therapy. And even those ministries which reach out to the community can become a mere easing of conscience for congregations troubled about their otherwise self-indulgent practices.

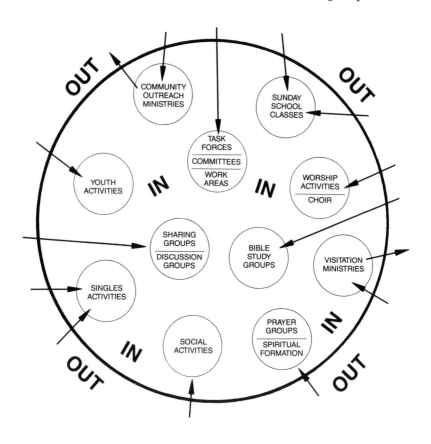

FIGURE 5: MINISTRIES OF ASSIMILATION

THE PRICE EXACTED BY CHURCH SAFE HOUSES

The people who pay most of the price for these safe houses are church leaders, both clergy and laity. In larger congregations, they are likely to be paid staff. Indeed, the size of a large church staff is often directly proportionate to the demands made upon them by the members. In smaller congregations the burden is no less demanding, though here it is likely to be carried by an overworked pastor and the few laity who are willing to share the responsibility. Having declared that the church is primarily a place where people can be helped, it is not surprising that they find themselves caught up in a round of activities which rapidly exhausts their energies and enervates their calling and vision.

Clearly this sort of congregational life bears little resemblance to God's mission in the world. It is not why men and women dedicate their lives and change their careers in order to serve the church. It is not why clergy submit to rigorous biblical and theological training in order to plumb the depths of Christian faith and understanding. And it is not why laity give countless hours to the stewardship of their church, spending valuable days at annual conferences and precious family time at committee meetings and workshops.

SIGNS OF FAITHFULNESS

All of this enculturation notwithstanding, countless laity remain faithful in such congregations, and countless clergy remain faithful in such pastorates. What is more, in many instances concerted efforts are being made to direct congregations away from the General Rule of Pastoral Prudence (the minimum in obligations in order to keep the maximum numbers) and toward the General Rule of Discipleship (acts of compassion, justice, worship, and devotion). In The United Methodist Church alone, there is a wealth of resources for all of these dimensions of Christian discipleship. There are ministries of outreach to the poor and disadvantaged; there are bold stands being made on issues of social justice; there is rich liturgical life, with a new United Methodist hymnal, destined to become a classic; and there are movements of spiritual renewal touching thousands of lives, especially in the area of Bible study.[18]

These ministries are impacting many local congregations and involving them more directly in God's mission to the world. Indeed, there are instances where the entire shape of a congregation's life and work has been changed by one or more of these reforming and renewing movements throughout the church.

A RADICAL INVERSION

With such plentiful signs of faithfulness, it would seem to be only a matter of time before the church as a whole should resume its proper role as messenger and herald of the coming reign of God. There is, however, a further step to take, and it is a radical step. For even when a congregation jettisons the General Rule of Pastoral Prudence and centers instead on the General Rule of Discipleship, in part or in whole, the pitfall of self-preoccupation can still be a danger. The community that is meant to be a sign of *shalom* for the world can still be more concerned with how good a sign it is than with how well it is pointing to the coming reign of God. The church can still be so concerned about how it is developing its discipleship that it fails to honor the Christ whose disciples it endeavors to be.

How, then, do we reliably avoid this pitfall? The answer lies in a total inversion of congregational identity. Faithful Christian disciples in vital congregations must accept and affirm that in God's plan of salvation *the church comes last, not first.* Jesus said as much (Matt. 19:30; Mark 10:44). The church does not exist for itself, or for its members, but for the *world.* And why is this? Because Jesus Christ died for the *world*—which is also where the Holy Spirit is at work.

CONGREGATIONS INSIDE OUT

Those of us who are committed to our discipleship and to our congregations may well have found this chapter disturbing, or even offensive. Let it quickly be said, therefore, that the preceding pattern of church "safe houses" is not a representation of particular congregations, but rather of an attitude into which any congregation may slip at one time or another—or perhaps with some regularity. Self-preoccupation is a constant pitfall for congregations in our present North American culture, and we must be ready to avoid it, and if need be, resist it. We must intentionally adopt an attitude that is quite the opposite of the "safe house."

Put another way, congregations must turn themselves inside out if they are to function as sign communities of the coming reign of God. They must exercise a ministry which allows the transforming grace of God to flow through their life and work into the world. Instead of places where people primarily come to be helped and served, they must be viewed as places where people primarily are empowered to serve Jesus Christ—in the world. Instead of discipleship being a mindset, obtained and sustained by intensive churchly activity, it must be viewed as a lifestyle which can be exercised only by intensive worldly activity. Instead of congregational vitality being viewed as large numbers of people flocking to church, it must be viewed as the sending of great clouds of witnesses into the world to challenge human sin with the power of the gospel.

The General Rule of Discipleship can shape the ministry of such congregations, so that the members will be formed as Christ's faithful disciples. They will be faithful evangelists, messengers of God to the world with the good news of forgiveness and reconciliation through Jesus Christ and transforming redemption through the Holy Spirit. They will be faithful stewards of God's creation, respecting every dimension of life on planet earth, and ready to give an account to God of how they have used their gifts and graces in service of Jesus Christ. They will be faithful teachers of God's Word, *handing over* to the world the good news of God's salvation in Christ, and *handing on* this tradition within the life and work of the church.

But first, they must become faithful disciples. They must not take the General Rule of Discipleship as an end in itself, but as the means to an end. They must center their discipleship, not on their church, not on their works, not even on their faith, but on the risen Christ, present through the Holy Spirit in every dimension of their lives.

For this to happen, not only must congregations be turned inside out. They must also be centered on Jesus Christ.

Chapter Three
Christ-Centered Congregations

CHRIST THE CENTER

The first thing to note about a Christ-centered congregation (Figure 6, following page) is that Christ is indeed at the center. This may seem an obvious statement to make, but in fact it is the most important point of all. For only when a congregation seeks to give honor to Christ in all things will the pitfall of self-preoccupation be avoided. Only when disciples of Christ seek to obey him in all things will the pitfall of self-gratification be avoided. The General Rule of Discipleship states this very clearly:

To witness to Jesus Christ in the world,
and to follow his teachings through
acts of compassion, justice, worship, and devotion,
under the guidance of the Holy Spirit.

Even so, countless congregations fill their weekly calendars with programs and activities which do not have Christ at the center. This is not to say that everything which takes place in our churches must be overtly spiritual. But it is to say that persons who visit our worship services, sample our programs, or merely come on to our premises, should quickly sense in whose name and for the sake of whose gospel we are gathered.

HESITANT WITNESS

Some of us hesitate to be so direct in our witness to Jesus Christ. At times this is prompted by the courtesy of not wishing to impose one's own views on others—a courtesy reinforced by our negative reaction to the aggressive tactics of certain kinds of "evangelism." More often, however, it stems from the attitudes fostered by our church "safe houses." With so many different ways of talking about God, and with so many congregations and denominations from which to choose, each with a multiplicity of programs, what right have we to advocate our particular beliefs over others? Why not let people find out for themselves what they wish to believe?

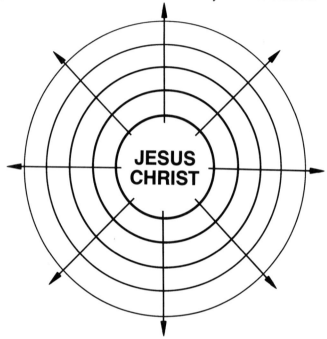

FIGURE 6: THE CHRIST-CENTERED CONGREGATION

There could be no greater indictment of our present-day approach to Christian discipleship and congregational life. It demonstrates with devastating clarity how we have removed Christ from center stage and replaced him with *our* beliefs, *our* perceptions, *our* intentions, and *our* activities. Little wonder we hesitate to advocate these concerns with anything like conviction. After all, it is only on a good day that we are sure about them ourselves.

By contrast, when Christ is at the center of our ministry, and the mission in which we are engaged is God's mission, there is no need for options, or choices, or beating about the bush. The task is so overwhelmingly obvious that Christians of every persuasion, whatever their stage of faith, whatever their talents, will be impelled to engage in faithful discipleship. Nor will they have any qualms about declaring in whose name and by whose grace they are about their business.

WHY WAS I NOT TOLD?

This registered with me some years ago, when a lawyer friend told me of his experience in a Third World country. He had been a Methodist all his life, and was then attending a large suburban congregation where the preaching was good, the worship was inspiring, the church school was well attended, the midweek programs were instructive, the outreach was commendable, and the membership visitation was efficient—the very paradigm, it would seem, of a vital congregation.

Then he went to Latin America to gather some information for a corporate lawsuit, and came back so angry that he spent a whole evening telling me how he felt.

"For the first time in my life, I have seen poverty firsthand. I have seen people living on top of open sewers, and under pieces of tin. I have seen children selling themselves so that their families might eat. I have seen women in their twenties already in old age. And I am very, very angry."

"At whom are you angry?" I responded.

"At first, I was angry at God, for claiming to be our heavenly Father, yet allowing all this to happen to little children. Then I was angry with myself, for being who I am—well fed, well housed, and well paid. But then I became angry with my church. Why did no one tell me that when Jesus said we should help the poor, he meant exactly that? Why did no one tell me that for rich people to complain about their "poverty of spirit" is an obscenity when people are living and dying as I have just seen them? Why do we have sermons assuring us week by week that Jesus loves us and wants to help us with our problems, when so many of our problems are caused by having too much wealth and too much freedom? And why do we so often make Jesus our errand boy, asking him to help the poor, when we are the ones who ought to be doing it?"

Since then, my friend has involved himself in significant ways with ministries to those in need, and has become a major civic leader in advocating justice for the poor. But I shall never forget his anger. He had come to experience what John Wesley called "the repentance of believers"—a quantum leap forward in his relationship with Jesus Christ that impelled him to a much more active discipleship. Yet he was angry that his congregation had fallen so heavily into the pitfall of self-preoccupation that he had to go to another country to meet Christ and be shown what really needs doing in the world.

Had Christ been at the center of his congregation's life and work, the task would have been so obvious that people like my friend would have "repented" much, much sooner.

NO BARRIERS

This story brings us to the next characteristic of a Christ-centered congregation: There are no barriers. The diagram in Figure 6 (p. 38) does not have a boundary at its perimeter to separate it from the world. There is no threshold to be crossed, and therefore no need for "points of entry." At its outer limits the Christ-centered congregation is indistinguishable from the rest of the world. It mingles with the world; it is firmly in and of the world.

THE SHAPE OF JESUS' MINISTRY

The reason for this is the person of Jesus Christ and the nature of his ministry. First, as "the word made flesh," he was God's definitive declaration that human beings and planet earth are worth saving—and are salvageable. He became one of us in every way. For God to take this initiative and assume human form means that followers of Jesus Christ can never reverse the initiative and seek to put a barrier between themselves and the world.

The shape of Jesus' ministry on earth is no less a factor. He went out of his way to be with ordinary people, and especially the people who were neglected or despised by everyone else (Matt. 9:10; Mark 5:25-34; Luke 19:1-10; John 8:3-11). He was much more concerned about the sinners and the outcasts than about the righteous, religious people of his day (Matt. 9:13; Mark 2:17; Luke 5:32).

A WARNING TO RELIGIOUS LEADERS

Indeed, it was the religious leaders of the day who criticized Jesus most sharply, and for whom he in turn reserved his harshest censure (Matt. 23:25-36; Mark 12:38-40). This should serve as a constant warning, not only for those of us who serve the church professionally, but for all of us who are committed to Christian discipleship—though not for the reason we might surmise. Before we censure the Sadducees and the Pharisees and the other religious leaders, we should look more carefully at their background.

When we read a little of their history, especially during the years between the Old and New Testaments, we find that these leaders were often at the forefront of the struggle to retain Jewish tradition and identity. They may have engaged in bouts of self-destructive rivalry, and the strength of their beliefs may have dragged them into religious bigotry. But they resisted the encroachment of other religions when many did not; and they suffered cruelly for their stand against foreign occupations, most notably under the Greeks and the Romans.

UNAPPRECIATED FAITHFULNESS

A moment's reflection should tell us that church leaders of today have one thing very much in common with these religious leaders of Jesus' day. Both they and we know what it means to hold fast to religious beliefs and stand firm in religious practices when the rest of society, and even the rest of the church, may not appreciate what we are doing. If the Pharisees and Sadducees separated themselves from the rest of the people, it was not necessarily because they sought social respect: They and their forebears had been denied that respect all too often. They stood apart in large measure because they had come to mistrust the commitment of ordinary people to their covenant tradition.

By the same token, those of us who take our beliefs and our leadership responsibilities seriously today are often rebuffed by our enculturated North American church, to say nothing of society at large. We are rarely persecuted; but we experience rejection often enough to cause a defensive reaction, especially if we have made any real effort to witness to Jesus Christ or to stand for God's justice. The fact of the matter is that the world in which we live is still not the kingdom of God. It is still resistant to God's grace and to the gospel of salvation. Likewise there are times when the church falls very short of being the sign community of the coming reign of God, leaving those of us who are trying to provide some leadership feeling isolated and rejected.

A WARNING NONETHELESS

The warning of Jesus rings loud and clear nonetheless: We are not to succumb to the pitfall of making our Christian discipleship *primarily* a means of comfort and support. When that happens, our congregations are quick to follow our signal, and become the church safe houses we censured so heavily in the previous chapter. They lose sight of their true identity and enter into the vicious circle of self-preoccupation, with all the ensuing demands on those of us who are leaders. It is then that we need a sharp reminder of what we ought truly to be about: helping Jesus Christ with the unfinished task of preparing for God's *shalom*.

CHOSEN FOR A PURPOSE

Perhaps this is why Jesus was so harsh with the Pharisees and Sadducees. In spite of all the sufferings they and their forebears and colleagues had endured, they had lost sight of their true identity as the chosen people of God:

> Thus says God, the Lord, who created the heavens
> and stretched them out,
> who spread out the earth and what comes from it,
> who gives breath to the people upon it and spirit
> to those who walk in it:
> I am the Lord, I have called you in righteousness,
> I have taken you by the hand and kept you;
> I have given you as a covenant to the people,
> a light to the nations,
> to open the eyes that are blind,
> to bring out the prisoners from the dungeon,
> from the prison those who sit in darkness.
>
> (Isa. 42:5-7)

God's purpose in calling the Hebrews into a covenant relationship was not for them to enjoy the blessings of a chosen people, even though they would receive such blessings in abundance. God's purpose rather was that they should be a means of blessing for the whole world, for all the families of the earth (Gen. 12:1-3). The identity of the church, the new Israel, is nothing less. We have been called into covenant by God for the sake of the world—to be a blessing and sign to the world.

GRACE FOR THE WORLD

Whether we are thanked, therefore, or rejected, we must place no barriers between the source of our grace and the rest of the world for whom that grace is intended. We receive our identity, not from setting ourselves apart from or over against the world, but rather from uniting ourselves with Jesus Christ. Joining this sort of congregation does not require the crossing of a threshold, but merely the desire to know the Christ who is self-evidently at the center of its life and work.

IN TOUCH WITH GOD'S GRACE IN THE WORLD

The next thing to note about a Christ-centered congregation is that it is in touch with what is really going on in the world. The universality of sin, evil, suffering, pain, and disease does not mean that God has abandoned the world. On the contrary, the Spirit of God is present throughout the world, ministering to every human being (Matt. 18:10-14) in every dimension of human existence (Rom. 13:1) and to every form of life (Luke 12:6). Just as human sin is personal, social, and systemic, so the Holy Spirit is at work in the lives of persons, societies, and systems.

When congregations see themselves as church safe houses, they find it difficult if not impossible to see the world in this way. So much of their attention is focused on themselves that they are unable to see God's grace at work elsewhere. This is an especially myopic perspective in the late twentieth century, when humankind has seen planet earth photographed from outer space, and when scientists are bringing us closer than ever to understanding the laws of time and energy by which God governs the universe.

THE "OPEN HOUSE" CHURCH

When congregations are centered on Jesus Christ, however, such vistas become clear to Christian disciples. Instead of safe houses seeking to separate themselves from the world, congregations are "open houses," seeking to be part of the world as it will be (Figure 7, following page). They glimpse the majestic sweep of God's creation, infinitely more wondrous than any human mind can comprehend. They see planet earth with new eyes—the eyes of Christ. They see a world which God loves, in spite of its waywardness; a world which God has covenanted to save, in spite of its sin; and a world in which God has undertaken to share our sin and suffering, so that we might be restored to the place in the cosmos we were created to enjoy.

GOD'S REVOLUTIONARY CITIZENSHIP

As we live out our discipleship in the world, we are not colonists for Christ, as has recently been suggested.[19] Rather we are bearers of a message of good news: that a new citizenship has been inaugurated for humankind, and a new order for planet earth. This is not a colonization, but a revolution: God's revolution. In contrast to all

worldly revolutions, this is a revolution in the true meaning of the
word: a turning back to God's original purpose for this planet.

Accordingly, the new citizenship has conditions: the goodwill
and the good behavior of universal *shalom*. There is no place in this
new worldly order for sinful habits and global bad manners; Jesus
Christ has made that very clear. We must therefore join him in the
struggle to bring God's revolution through to its triumphant conclusion. We must invite everyone to share in its privileges—and
caution everyone to live by its ground rules.

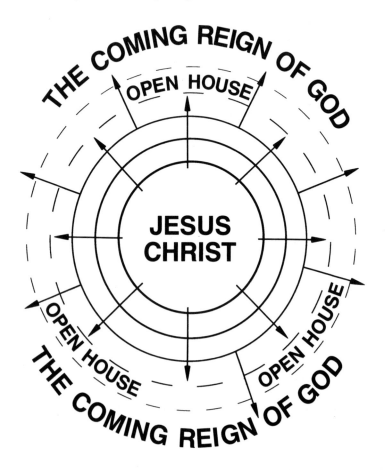

FIGURE 7: THE "OPEN HOUSE" CHURCH

AMBASSADORS FOR CHRIST

This is news so good that it should have us on the rooftops, resorting to wild eccentricities in order to get it heard. If such actions cause us embarrassment or humiliation, that is a small price to pay for the honor of being "ambassadors for Christ" (2 Cor. 5:20). And even if our witness should cause us persecution, suffering, or death, we will still be in the best of Christian company.

If the supreme privilege of Christian discipleship is that our eyes have been opened to God's revolution before it is complete, then our minimum obligation is to tell everyone about it: to assure everyone that the day is coming when God will open the eyes of all who are blind and bring out of the dungeons all who sit in darkness; to promise those who are sinned against that the day is coming when justice will roll down like waters; and to live in the world as exemplars of Jesus himself, following his teachings through acts of compassion, justice, worship, and devotion. When we are Christ-centered, we see that this is precisely what God is doing in the world through the power and the grace of the Holy Spirit, in countless ways and in countless lives.

WHY CHRIST-CENTERED CONGREGATIONS?

The presence of the Holy Spirit in the world, interacting with and reinforcing the witness of Christ-centered congregations, affirms the doctrine of the Trinity in a way that is never possible in church safe houses. It does, however, raise an interesting question. If the risen Christ is one with the Holy Spirit, and is therefore as much in the world as at the center of the church; and if, by the same token, the Holy Spirit is at the center of the church no less than anywhere else in the world; then why place Christ at the center of the church? Why not the Holy Spirit, or indeed, why not the triune God?

THE FORM OF DISCIPLESHIP

The question is much more important than it seems, and the answer lies in the General Rule of Discipleship: "To follow the teachings of Jesus Christ in the world." As we noted in Chapter 1, the Holy Spirit gives us the power to live out our discipleship; but it is Christ who gives us the *form*, the guidelines by which to live. Placing Christ at the center of our congregation means that the teachings of Jesus of Nazareth shape our discipleship (Figure 8, p. 46).

Unless we give full measure to these teachings, we risk the cardinal error of license, or self-indulgence; just as we risk the cardinal error of legalism if we try to follow the teachings of Jesus without the power of the Holy Spirit. Both the form and the power of discipleship are equally important.

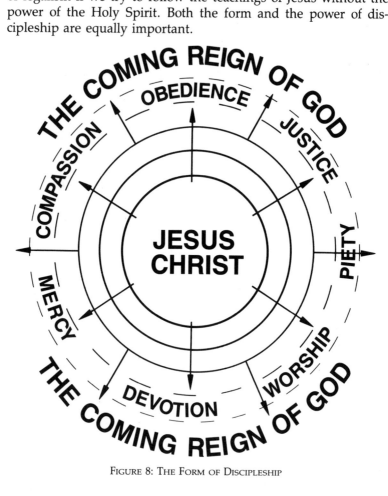

FIGURE 8: THE FORM OF DISCIPLESHIP

JESUS OUR ROLE MODEL

As human beings living in the world, our first consideration must be to pattern our lives according to our human role model, Jesus Christ. The Holy Spirit will then give us whatever power we need to sustain us. If this sequence is reversed, it is not long before we stumble into the pitfall of self-preoccupation. To commit our-

selves to Jesus Christ and place him at the center of our congregational life means that we go with him into the world, joining him in
ministry to his little ones. As we do so, we are affirmed and
empowered by the Holy Spirit, who is already there ahead of us.
And through the mystical union of the God who is three-in-one,
we find ourselves in ministry to Christ himself among the hungry,
the thirsty, the strangers, the naked, the sick, and the imprisoned
(Matt. 25:35-36). But if we place the Holy Spirit at the center of our
congregational life and work, seeking the grace and the power of
God before we even attempt to follow the teachings of Jesus, then
we begin to covet the benefits of discipleship before fulfilling our
obligations.

POWER THROUGH OBEDIENCE

The pitfall is subtle because, as we have noted, our discipleship
needs form and power in equal measure; besides which, Jesus
Christ and the Holy Spirit are co-equal persons within the Trinity.
But when we seek the power of God *before* we have honored God's
human form; when we seek to know Christ without first obeying
him; then we profoundly misunderstand the nature of our discipleship:

> Now by this we may be sure that we know him, if we obey his com-
> mandments. Whoever says, "I have come to know him," but does not
> obey his commandments, is a liar, and in such a person the truth does
> not exist; but whoever obeys his word, truly in this person the love of
> God has reached perfection. By this we may be sure that we are in him:
> whoever says, "I abide in him," ought to walk just as he walked (1 John
> 2:3-6).

LOVE THROUGH OBEDIENCE

It is possible to "spiritualize" this teaching of John, and interpret it
to mean that the love of God, imparted by the Holy Spirit, will
ultimately bring us to the point where we do in fact obey the
commandments of Jesus. But this is precisely the sort of effortless
discipleship spurned by Bonhoeffer and others as "cheap grace."[20]
At best it cuts the nerve of our commitment and gives us permission
to do less than our best for Christ. At worst, it reduces the awesome
drama of our salvation to the level of a soap opera which requires
nothing more from us than fleeting emotional involvement.

There is a profound sense in which the grace of God does indeed
hone and mature our discipleship. But it requires our participation,

our commitment, and our effort. It is not the love of God that perfects our obedience to Christ. *It is obedience to Christ that perfects our love of God.*

THE INTERACTION OF GRACE

Once Christian disciples experience the interaction of a Christ-centered congregation and a Spirit-filled world, it becomes clear there are no limits to the work of God's grace. Figure 9 illustrates how the presence of the Holy Spirit in the world invites, prompts, cajoles, and even pushes people to the place where they can encounter Jesus Christ. It shows in turn how the teachings of Jesus Christ, embodied in the congregation, are disseminated into the world through the grace and the power of the Holy Spirit at work in faithful Christian disciples.

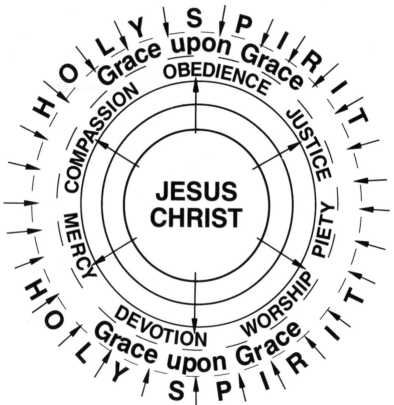

FIGURE 9: THE INTERACTION OF GRACE

The result is a constant interaction: the grace of God in the world, mediated by the Holy Spirit; and the grace of God in the church, mediated by Jesus Christ. Since there is no boundary or threshold to these open house congregations, people may seek Christ as the Spirit leads them; and since there is no outer perimeter, disciples of Christ may take his gospel into the world without hindrance or hesitation.

Moreover, the groups or subfamilies of the congregation, which in church safe houses are such a constant drain on time and resources, in church open houses become vital means of grace. Because of the dynamic interaction of grace, they are free to function in a wide range of contexts, moving in or out of the congregational setting wherever Christ sends them or the Holy Spirit invites them. Nor do they have to jostle for position in the churchly pecking order: They are far too concerned with the greater task of helping Christ to prepare for *shalom*.

THE FREEDOM OF CHRIST-CENTERED DISCIPLESHIP

This is a liberating concept, not only for our congregations, but also for our discipleship. As we noted in Chapters 1 and 2, a faith-centered discipleship will ultimately lead us into congregational self-preoccupation, where our concerns are the constant and Jesus Christ is the variable. This results in a highly flexible application of Jesus' teachings, as evidenced by the loose interpretation given to the word *discipleship*. But when Christ is at the center of our congregations, then his teachings are the constant and our concerns are the variable. Therein lies the freedom of authentic discipleship. With Christ and his teachings at the center of our ministry and mission, all are free to respond to Christ with whatever faith, whatever works, whatever degree of commitment the Holy Spirit gives them the grace to respond.

Thus the casual enquirer on a Sunday morning, or the parents and children doing their best to live as a Christian family, or the intellectual struggling with what it really means to make a commitment, or the dedicated Sunday school teacher quietly shaping the lives of young disciples, or the unassuming saint who has weathered countless spiritual battles, or the faithful prophet working for God's justice in the community, or the hard-pressed volunteer striving to stem the casualties of a society devoted to greed—all of these are making appropriate and acceptable responses to Jesus of

Nazareth. The mixture is rich, and the pattern of discipleship infinitely varied.

THE CAPTIVITY OF
FAITH-CENTERED DISCIPLESHIP

By contrast, when our response to Jesus Christ becomes the center of our discipleship rather than Christ himself, ironically we find ourselves increasingly drawn into an appalling blandness and homogeneity. This is difficult to comprehend, because so much of the language and so many of the programs of our self-preoccupied congregations seem to stress diversity and pluralism; and to some extent they do. But in the most critical area of all—our discipleship—they suffer from a serious and ultimately self-defeating limitation: they depend on *our* notion of discipleship, not that of Jesus Christ; on *our* ideas about the coming reign of God, not those of Jesus Christ; on *our* concepts of faith and commitment, not those of Jesus Christ; and on giving people options for Christian living which are not options at all—because *we* have determined the options, not Jesus Christ.

PROGRESSIVE BLANDNESS AND HOMOGENEITY

The viciousness of this circle is that our discipleship becomes ever more bland as we seek to enrich it, and ever more self-centered as we endeavor to live it out in the world. Each time we seek guidance in Christian living, but focus on what this will do for our faith in Christ rather than what it will do to serve Christ, we end up with a compass heading which is even more introspective than the last. The result is that we find ourselves uniformly without direction and without purpose.

As long as the objective is to strengthen *our* faith, to deepen *our* spirituality, to utilize *our* gifts, or to fulfill *our* potential, there will be a progressive homogenization of our congregational life. The smorgasbord of our programs may appear to indicate sensitivity to the wide range of faith and commitment which comprise the average congregation; yet in fact we present only one basic criterion— the meeting of personal needs. The options we offer are merely cosmetic.

RICHNESS AND DIVERSITY

But once the objective of a congregation is to follow Jesus Christ, and to serve under his leadership in preparing for *shalom*, it will encompass the widest possible spectrum of response to his call. Its members will include those who are ready to lay down their lives for the coming reign of God, those who are tentatively considering a visit to Christ in secret by night, and everyone in between. An infinitely rich and profoundly diverse range of discipleship develops in a congregation centered on Jesus Christ. For when Christ truly is the head, all parts of the body are free to be themselves—to be fully Christ's eyes and ears and hands and feet.

QUESTIONS OF CHURCH MEMBERSHIP

At this point, the open house model of the congregation is bound to raise some pressing questions about church membership. For example, does the absence of a clear boundary at the outer perimeter of congregation mean that there should be no distinction at all between the church and the world? Does the open invitation into the fellowship of the church mean that membership vows are meaningless? If these vows are significant, at what point in the dynamic interaction between Christ-centered congregation and Spirit-filled world should people be asked to take them? Indeed, if the benefits and obligations of God's grace are available to anyone and everyone through these open house congregations, why should membership vows be taken at all? Does such a model of the church, albeit Christ-centered and Spirit-filled, leave Christians with any real bedrock for their faith?

These are valid questions, and they must be answered. For if faithful discipleship requires both form and power, no less do vital congregations require right doctrine and disciplinary structure as well as spiritual energy and activity. The earliest Christians quickly discovered this, as the letters of Paul make clear. Christian discipleship must be accountable to the Christian community; and the community in turn must be accountable to established teaching and practice. The waywardness of human nature, to say nothing of the unpredictability of a world not yet subject to the reign of God, renders such accountability indispensable.

THE GENERAL RULE OF DISCIPLESHIP

The answer to these questions is once again to be found in the General Rule of Discipleship and the scriptures from which it is drawn. In addition to following the teachings of Jesus through acts of compassion, justice, worship, and devotion, the General Rule states that Christian disciples should witness to Jesus Christ in the world. In other words, the teachings of Jesus Christ must be complemented by the teachings of the church.

On the one hand, the teachings of Jesus provide us with guidelines for faithful Christian living in the world. On the other hand, the teachings of the church provide us with guidelines for our witness to Jesus Christ as Savior of the world and Sovereign of the coming reign of God. Faithful disciples follow the teachings *about* Jesus no less than the teachings *of* Jesus.

THE TEACHINGS OF THE CHURCH

The teachings of the church about Jesus are summarized in the creeds that have formulated the corporate testimonies about Jesus since the earliest days of Christianity. Many of these creedal statements were originally associated with the catechesis of the church—a question-and-answer form of instruction for new members and for children being instructed in the faith.[21] Just as discipleship is severely impaired when these creedal statements are made the focus of discipleship to the detriment of faithful Christian living in the world, so discipleship is severely impaired when efforts are made to follow the teachings of Jesus without witnessing to his person. The church affirms that Jesus of Nazareth is:

> [God's] only Son, our Lord,
> (Mark 1:1; Rom. 1:4)
>
> who was conceived by the Holy Spirit,
> (Matt. 1:18-21)
>
> born of the Virgin Mary,
> (Isa. 7:14; Luke 1:26-35)
>
> suffered under Pontius Pilate,
> (Mark 15:1-15; John 18:28–19:16)
>
> was crucified, died, and was buried;
> (Matt. 27:32-66; John 19:16-42)
>
> he descended to the dead.
> (Psa. 139:8; Acts 2:31; Rev. 1:18)
>
> On the third day he rose again;
> (Mark 16:1-8; 1 Cor. 15:4)
>
> he ascended into heaven,
> (Luke 24:50-53; Acts 1:6-11)

is seated at the right hand of the Father,
(Mark 16:19; Acts 2:33)

and will come again to judge the living and the dead.
(2 Tim. 4:1; 1 Pet. 4:5)

FORMING A RELATIONSHIP WITH JESUS

There are few persons whose initial encounter with this Christ is dramatic—whose repentance and conversion are radical and sudden. For the great majority of us, whether or not we have had a Christian background or upbringing, our involvement with Jesus of Nazareth grows over a period of time. There are critical points in this process, most especially when we first accept for ourselves the identity of Christian, and these are dealt with in more detail in the companion volume, *Class Leaders*. But over the years, our relationship with Christ is one that grows and develops, just as it did for the first disciples.

When congregations are Christ-centered, this growth takes place by the grace of the Holy Spirit rather than by human design or intent. People are drawn to Christ according to God's purpose, not ours. The church open house permits these introductions to be made with courtesy and good manners rather than by maneuvering or pressure—much the same as Jesus himself dealt with people.

STAGES OF COMMITMENT

In the church "open house," the point at which persons are ready to join the church by baptism, or are ready to profess their faith in Jesus Christ as Savior and Lord, or experience the "new birth" through the inward witness of the Holy Spirit, or are ready to take membership training and vows, or are willing to make further commitments in their discipleship—all of these stages of commitment emerge quite naturally in the breadth and openness of a Christ-centered community. The church "open house" does not compromise commitment to Christ or church membership vows. On the contrary, it gives them full integrity, in that people are welcomed into the fellowship of the congregation *at whatever stage of faith they happen to be*, and *at whatever level of commitment they are ready to make*. The difference is that, whereas in the church "safe house" these steps of faith are viewed as thresholds, and may even become barriers, in the church "open house" they become encounters of grace (see Figure 10, p. 54), in which persons who have been invited and impelled by the Holy Spirit meet with the Risen Christ who is waiting to welcome them as his disciples.

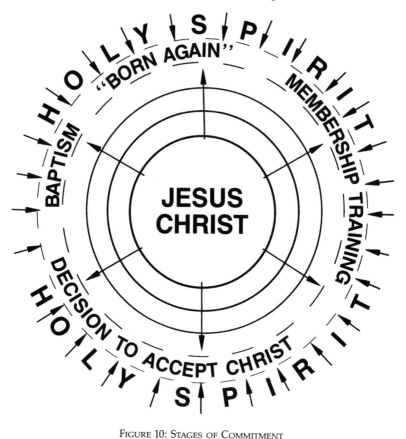

FIGURE 10: STAGES OF COMMITMENT

CHRIST MUST BE AT THE CENTER

The all-important proviso, of course, is that Christ must be at the center of the congregation, both to shape its ministry and mission, and to shape the discipleship of its members. A living relationship with Christ and an obedience to him in the world are of paramount importance. Anything else makes the church open house even worse than the safe house; for at least in the safe house there is a clear statement of identity, a clear distinction between the church and the world. If Christ is not at the center of the church open house, however, then there is nothing to prevent it from being totally absorbed into its cultural context.

THREE OPEN HOUSE ERRORS

Sometimes we find open house congregations trying to shape their mission and form their discipleship without placing Christ at the center. Figure 11 illustrates three of these erroneous attempts:

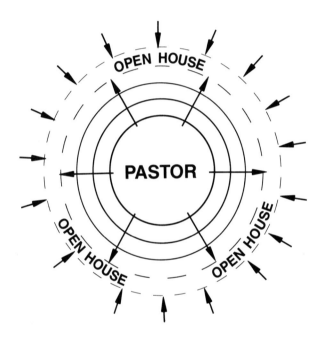

FIGURE 11A

1. Pastor-Centered Congregations

One mistake is to place the pastor at the center and focus everything on her or his ministry. It is especially apt to happen when the pastor is an outstanding preacher, scholar, counselor, or organizer. To say that this is a mistake is not an argument against strong pastoral leadership *per se;* but when the pastor occupies a central role, it becomes increasingly difficult for him or her to be responsive to the demands of the congregation, and at the same time remain faithful to the gospel. Enculturation is almost inevitable.

2. Program-Centered Congregations

Another error is to place programming at the center of a congregation. Once again the error is not in the programs *per se,* but in giving them a primary role. When this happens in a church open house, the congregation merely adopts the criteria of a safe house, though with fewer membership restrictions; and it then becomes difficult to maintain even a programmatic focus. For by their very nature, programs are centrifugal. They will gravitate out into the congregation, leaving a vacuum at the center that will quickly lead to enculturation. It will also lead to extreme overwork for the staff. In a church open house, they do not have the advantage of a clear perimeter to their pastoral constituency, and are thereby forced to rely on the quality of their programs in order to recruit and retain their membership—a peculiarly North American version of the Rule of Pastoral Prudence.[22]

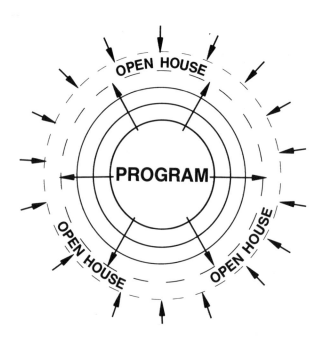

FIGURE 11B

3. Church-Centered Congregations

A third error is that of placing the church itself at the center of the congregation. In some aspects this is a form of the church safe house, but there is a critical difference. The church-centered congregation is less preoccupied with the needs of its members than with what they all have accomplished. Thus, the buildings, the programs, the budget, the pastor, even the members themselves, become means of extolling the work of the church. Such a congregation is particularly vulnerable to any changes in its social or cultural context, since it lacks the clear boundary of a church safe house, and only incidentally does it witness to Jesus Christ.

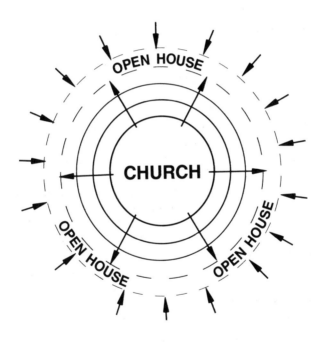

FIGURE 11c

LACK OF IDENTITY

None of these substitute centers provides a proper identity for such congregations. Ultimately they become church safe houses and slip into the pitfall of self-preoccupation where so many congregations in the United States find themselves today. As we have noted, these safe houses can be found at every point of the theological spectrum. Whether they regard the boundary they place between themselves and the world as the distinction between "saved" and "unsaved," or as the threshold of a membership with deeply sacramental significance, or as the entry into a community of transforming relationships, none of these separations from the world is an acceptable form of the church of Jesus Christ, called to be the light and salt of the world, and the seed and leaven of *shalom.*

HOW TO BECOME CHRIST-CENTERED

The only true identity for a congregation is to be a sign community of the coming reign of God. And the only way to sustain this identity and to avoid the pitfall of self-preoccupation is to be centered on Jesus Christ. The pivotal question therefore becomes, How does a congregation ensure that Christ is indeed at the center of its ministry and mission?

The answer, as might be expected, is to be found in the New Testament. When Jesus was ready to begin his public ministry, he first called his disciples (Matt. 4:18-22; Mark 1:16-20; Luke 5:1-11). There were a number of reasons for taking such a step, not least of which was the continuation of his work after his death. But during his ministry in Galilee and Judea, it became clear that his disciples were vitally important in three other ways: They provided companionship and support for Jesus in his ministry (Matt. 12:46-50; John 6:1-14); they gave him an intimate context for his deepest teachings (Matt. 26:26-29; Mark 4:34, 8:31-33; Luke 22:14-20); and they witnessed to him throughout the land (Matt. 10:5-15; Luke 19:29-40). Thus, if people wanted to learn about Jesus of Nazareth, to inquire into his teachings, or merely to know where he could be found, they would first ask one of his disciples.

WHERE ARE THE DISCIPLES TODAY?

The same is true today. If anyone wishes to know about Jesus of Nazareth, to learn about his teachings, or to meet him personally, Christian disciples are the ones to ask first. The question then becomes, Where are these disciples in the church of today?

Once we pose this further question, we see even more clearly the extent to which a faith-centered approach to discipleship and a safe house approach to congregational identity place the church at a severe disadvantage. Faith-centered disciples are able to say much about what Christ has done for them, but little about Christ himself. Congregational safe houses have much of themselves to offer, but little of what Christ has to offer. In fact, the more one gets to know a "faith-centered" disciple or a safe house congregation, the more difficult it often becomes to find the Jesus of Nazareth whose name they both claim to honor.

NO AGREED CRITERIA

As we have already noted, the problem is that when Christ has been made the variable, our response to Christ becomes the constant. In a congregational safe house, this translates into the substantial handicap of no agreed criteria for faithful discipleship. In such a setting, Christ has as many forms as he has disciples. The only condition for discipleship is assent to or belief in a Christ who is as vague and as varied as a congregation's range of personal faith. And since personal faith is by definition extremely personal, no one is entitled to inquire into how members of a congregation are living out their faith: whether they might need encouragement or support; and just as important, whether they might need reproof or correction.

NO RECOGNIZED LEADERS

By the same token, and even more detrimental to the ministry and mission of the church, this congregational handicap prevents the recognition of those members who have the potential for leading in discipleship. Just as Jesus of Nazareth called a few to be his disciples in order that they might perpetuate and extend his ministry to the people at large, so the risen Christ calls a few church members today to follow him with more accountability so that his ongoing ministry might be extended throughout our congregations, and thence to the world.

Failure to recognize such persons is the foremost cause of congregational self-preoccupation, and in turn of personal self-gratification in the Christian life. It means the absence of any true role models for discipleship, and thus of any feasible method for the forming of Christian disciples. It also means that the leadership of a congregation is viewed primarily in terms of pastoral staff, program, and administration—precisely the errors we have just identified as unacceptable.

LEADERS IN DISCIPLESHIP

To ensure that a congregation is centered on Christ, rather than on these ultimately self-defeating alternatives, recognition must be given to those persons who are willing to make the necessary commitment and sacrifice to an intentional, accountable discipleship. Figure 12 illustrates the effect this has on the ministry and mission of a congregation. On the one hand, the General Rule of Discipleship is interpreted to the entire membership, and the teachings of Jesus Christ thus have the widest possible impact. On the other hand, as the grace of the Holy Spirit draws people into the sphere of such a congregation, they find persons with an

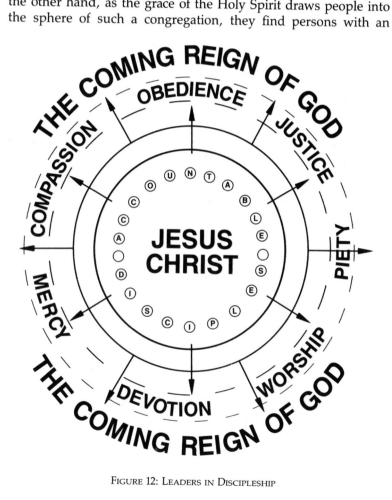

FIGURE 12: LEADERS IN DISCIPLESHIP

acknowledged leadership role whose concern is to make Christ the center of their own discipleship, and thus of the congregation as a whole.

Such leaders are always present in the church. Only in Christ-centered open houses, however, can they be recognized and commissioned for their proper role.

POTENTIAL CRITICISM

A leadership role such as this may well draw criticism within the congregation. Persons who assume such a position may be regarded as an elite cadre who claim to have the inside track with Christ—who are "holier than thou," or "super Christians," or "works righteous," or even "more saved" than everyone else. Leaders of any kind are likely to experience criticism from time to time. But in our present safe house climate, leaders in discipleship will be especially vulnerable to these disparagements, even when their role is understood.

Criticisms will probably lean toward the argument that no one has the right to judge anyone else's discipleship. This is true. But it is altogether mistaken to infer from this that no one has the right to *lead* another person in discipleship, or to *show* someone else how to be a disciple. A Christ-centered discipleship by definition requires role models, so that the teachings of Christ can provide the form of Christian living in the world along with the power of the Holy Spirit.

THE METHODIST TRADITION

While there is no sure safeguard against these criticisms, the Methodist tradition provides two leadership models which do more than most to answer them: the class meeting and the class leader. While both of these models have largely been abandoned by the church, or else have become pale reflections of what they once were, they have not disappeared altogether; and in some branches of Methodism beyond the United States, they are still vigorous.

Class meetings and class leaders provided our Methodist forebears with a means of forming a balanced discipleship and living it out faithfully in the world. As might be expected, they were criticized for their methodical ways. Indeed, their nickname of "Methodist" implies precisely the elitism attributed to those who take their discipleship seriously in our own day and age. Yet if our congregations are to be Christ-centered, we must weather such criticism, and focus instead on how to form such disciples again. The way to do this is to develop a new generation of leaders—leaders with integrity; and just as important, to gain their recognition by the membership of the church as a whole.

AN UNACCEPTABLE STATE OF AFFAIRS

The alternative to this will be a continuing preponderance of church safe houses with their various self-preoccupations. No amount of programming, strategizing, exhorting, or training will enable the pastoral staff of these congregations to form Christian disciples, for the simple reason that the natural leadership already present in the congregation will remain unrecognized and unemployed. And this, needless to say, would be a totally unacceptable state of affairs.

REAPPROPRIATING THE TRADITION

Accordingly, the General Board of Discipleship of The United Methodist Church has adopted *Covenant Discipleship Groups* and *Class Leaders* as churchwide initiatives in order to revitalize the Methodist tradition of strong lay leadership along with that of the clergy.

Covenant discipleship groups, patterned after the early Methodist class meeting, are designed for those members of a congregation who are ready to be accountable for their discipleship. As such, they provide a context for leadership in the congregation, not because they are thereby better Christians, still less because they are better persons. The difference is that they have made a commitment to be *accountable* for their walk with Christ, and are thus going to be effective role models in discipleship. In this respect they are like the first disciples of Jesus, who were not an exceptional group of persons, but were different in one crucial dimension of their lives: They left their nets and followed him.

While covenant discipleship groups develop this context for leadership in the congregation, class leaders make the leadership explicit. They are the laypersons who are given recognition by the congregation as leaders in discipleship—persons who will help to form the discipleship of a subgrouping of the church members. Their authority does not lie in their official recognition alone. It lies also in the fact that they are members of covenant discipleship groups, holding themselves accountable for their own discipleship before trying to help other people with theirs.

By no means everyone in a covenant discipleship group will be gifted for the office of class leader; nor will everyone wish to be a class leader. But the fact that everyone who is a class leader will belong to a covenant discipleship group gives the office a credibility which does not come from training, or from discernment of gifts and graces. Class leaders will have credibility because they will lead by example. Their weekly accountability in a covenant discipleship group means that they will not be asking anyone else to do what they themselves are not already doing. Their leadership will consist of a practical sharing of the basics of Christian discipleship with others—a "showing of the ropes."

CO-PASTORAL LEADERSHIP

Figure 13, page 64, illustrates how covenant discipleship groups and class leaders work with the pastor in forming Christian disciples and in giving the congregation a Christ-centered leadership. In a real sense, class leaders are co-pastors of the congregation. When the office of class leader is adopted or revitalized by a congregation, pastors fulfill their role in a very different way. They become facilitators of a pastoral team; and for many clergy, this means a whole new approach to their ministry. To describe Christ-centered congregations as "inverted," therefore, is no exaggeration. With new leadership roles, new understandings of discipleship, and new visions of what they can do to work with Christ in preparing for *shalom* in the world, congregations such as these are indeed turned inside out.

The two companion volumes, *Covenant Discipleship* (order no. DR091B) and *Class Leaders* (order no. DR092B), explain in detail how to implement these two models of leadership: how to form and sustain covenant discipleship groups, and how to appoint and work with class leaders. The remainder of this volume explains how they can both be incorporated into the life and work of the congregation.

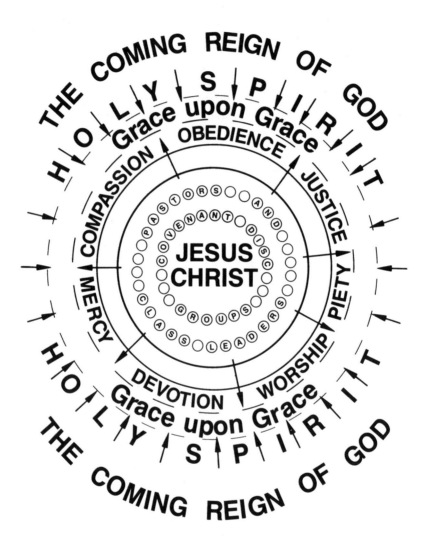

FIGURE 13: COVENANT DISCIPLESHIP AND CLASS LEADERS
IN THE CONGREGATION

PART TWO

Covenant Discipleship Groups in the Congregation

A covenant discipleship group consists of up to seven people who agree to meet together for one hour per week in order to hold themselves mutually accountable for their discipleship. They do this by affirming a written covenant on which they themselves have agreed.

Chapter Four

Introducing Covenant Discipleship

The name *Covenant Discipleship* comprises two of the most important words in the life and work of the church, and it will be helpful at the outset to look at each of them in turn and see how they are related.

"COVENANT"

The idea of *covenant* is the central theme of the Bible, and a watchword for the identity of the church. It appears in scripture with a number of connotations. There is first of all the covenant which God has made with the whole of humankind, the covenant of forgiveness and reconciliation. This has been made supremely in and through Jesus Christ, the Savior of the world. Then there is the covenant which God makes with those of us who are called into a particular relationship with Jesus Christ. This is a relationship with a purpose—to help the risen Christ with the unfinished work of salvation in the world, as the Holy Spirit brings God's love, peace, and justice to fulfillment in human history. Third, there are the covenants which Christian disciples make with each other as they endeavor to perform their service faithfully.

There are several things we should note about these various covenants:

- They are all at God's initiative. Our contribution to them is one of response. In other words, they are *gracious* covenants, even the covenants we make with each other. The Old and New Testaments are quite adamant on this point: No covenant is possible without the grace of God (Gen. 6:18; Ex. 6:4; Jer. 31:31-34; Heb. 10:16).

- God is always faithful in covenant; usually we are not. Time and again we read in scripture that the people of God broke their covenant (Jer. 11:10; Hos. 6:7). Those of us in the church have hardly improved on their performance. Yet God remains steadfast, and patiently waits for us to be more faithful. That is why there must never be any compromise of *intent* on our part, however inconsistent we might be in fulfilling our covenant obligations (Ps. 25:10; 103:17-18).

• Temporary arrangements have no place here. God's covenants are always permanent (Lev. 24:8; Isa. 55:3; Heb. 13:20). The least we can do, therefore, is to *try* to be faithful. The short-term agreements so popular in the church of today (supposedly to persuade or motivate us into something more permanent when we find it convenient) are a serious compromise and are rarely effective. To be in covenant with God may be convenient for us, but in fact, it is often an inconvenience. That is why short-term "covenants" of planned obsolescence are a misuse of the word.

• The covenants we make with each other are primarily to help us keep our covenant with God. The reason for this is that we live in a world which has yet to accept God's offer of salvation. We constantly face temptations to turn away from God. Therefore we need some means of mutual support. John Wesley understood this need, and saw that nothing short of mutual covenant would suffice—a "watching over one another in love" (Heb. 10:23-25; 1 John 4:7-21).

"DISCIPLESHIP"

This second word is the key to understanding the first. For if our covenants mean anything at all, with God or with each other, we must do everything in our power to keep them. The grace of God is the primary source for this power, but we too have a part to play. We must *allow* God's grace to work in our lives, and we must *accept* God's conditions. In short, to enter into covenant is to accept a *disciplined* agreement.

As we noted in Chapter 1, the origin of the word *disciple* is the Latin word *discipulus,* meaning a student who was willing to make a total commitment to a particular teacher in order to learn. This may not have been a literal "sitting at the feet" of the teacher all of the time, but it was the closest of bonds. It was to spend a great deal of time with the teacher, and to follow as faithfully as possible the practical implications of the teacher's thought and example.

THE NEW TESTAMENT MODEL

This is the model we have in the New Testament. Jesus called his disciples to follow him in person, wherever he went, whatever he did. As they walked and talked together, they learned from him. In fact, they learned more than they knew, because it was only after his death and resurrection that they came to understand many of his teachings and his actions. The only way they could have done this was by sacrificing other priorities—their work, their families, their friends. And this, as we know, is exactly what they did.

Today we use the word *disciple* much more loosely. We tend to apply it to anyone who has accepted Jesus Christ as Savior and Lord, overlooking the fact that this does not necessarily make of a person the disciplined follower described in the New Testament. In many of our congregations, "disciples" would more aptly describe the much larger company who followed Jesus, often from a distance or in the crowds. They listened to his parables; they came to be healed and fed; many of them even accepted his teachings; but not many of them accepted the more demanding role of disciple.

THE "MUSCLE" OF THE CHURCH

There are always those, however, who are ready to accept this more demanding role; and covenant discipleship groups are designed for such persons—to equip them for their role and to give them a clear identity in the mission and ministry of the congregation. This is done through a weekly time of mutual accountability: one hour, spent in telling other persons of like mind and purpose how they have journeyed as a Christian disciple during the past week. It involves a degree of self-evaluation; but much more important, it imparts the sense of a shared journey. Telling trusted colleagues how we have fared along the way helps us in our own pilgrimage as we learn from each other how to be more seasoned travelers.

A good way to describe these accountable disciples is that they are the "muscle" of the church—those who give the congregation a binding and a strength for its task in the world. Our congregations have this "muscle"; but by and large they have not been using it. Covenant discipleship groups are a way of "tuning" it again.

COVENANT DISCIPLESHIP IS VOCATIONAL

Just as muscle does not make up the whole body, so it should not be expected that every member of a congregation will wish to make a commitment to a covenant discipleship group. If this seems surprising, given that the disciplines of the groups are really quite minimal, then it must be remembered that people respond to God's grace with varying degrees of commitment, and with varying degrees of faith.

There is nothing in a covenant of discipleship that a person does not promise to be and to do when joining the church. But the extent to which this commitment is lived out, or even understood, will depend on the stage of a person's faith and the point he or she has reached in pilgrimage with Christ. The essential dynamic of Christian discipleship is our response to grace; and while Christ remains constant, disciples of Christ manifest a very wide range of response.

This has been confirmed by the many congregations that have adopted the groups during the past ten years. When the recommended procedures have been followed, a remarkably consistent statistic has emerged: Some 15 percent of the active membership (i.e., the number of members regularly at worship) are ready to take part in a covenant discipleship group. This means that somewhere between 5 and 7 percent of the members are ready to be held accountable for their discipleship—a figure that tends to reflect the statistics for spiritual commitment in the nation as a whole (see above, p. 11).

OPEN TO EVERYONE

This does not mean, however, that the opportunity to join a covenant discipleship group should not be given to all church members—and given repeatedly. The seminal work in the area of faith development by James W. Fowler is directly affirming of Wesley's remarkable understanding of religious vocation: that it is progressive, with each stage having its own integrity.[23] It follows that church members will wish to make a deeper commitment to their faith at certain points in their pilgrimage, and should feel free to do so in the environment of their local congregation.

Covenant discipleship groups have proved to be an excellent way of keeping such vocational steps constantly available, providing not only the opportunity to commit to Christian discipleship, but also to further that commitment. This is explained in more detail in the companion volume, *Covenant Discipleship.*

TWO CAUTIONARY WORDS

Before describing the introduction of groups into the congregation, there are two cautionary words about covenant discipleship, both of them extremely important. The first concerns the role of the pastor, and the second concerns the length of the commitment being made by the members.

THE ROLE OF THE PASTOR

Pivotal to the success or failure of covenant discipleship groups is the role of the pastor, who must be convinced of their value and validity if they are to have anything to contribute to the ministry and mission of a congregation. This is not to imply that the groups require intensive pastoral supervision. On the contrary, one of their strengths is that they quickly become self-supervising and self-supporting. But if they are to be integral to the life and work of the church, the pastor must be certain of their function in relation to everything else which takes place in the congregation.

By the same token, if the pastor is not convinced of the validity of covenant discipleship groups, there is little likelihood of their becoming effective in a congregation. Through preaching, through pastoral care, through the countless private conversations and public exchanges in which a pastor shares, the concept of covenant discipleship can be approved or disdained, affirmed or denied. This is why, as we shall presently observe, it is vitally important that the pastor be a member of the first group to be formed.

OPENENDED COMMITMENT

The second cautionary word concerns the nature of commitment to covenant discipleship. Those who join a group should understand that their commitment is openended—most likely for the remainder of their Christian life. If there is a distinguishing characteristic of covenant discipleship, this is it. To join a covenant discipleship group is not to exercise a preference, but to respond to a call; and group members need to understand this at the outset, so that they in turn can affirm it for the rest of the congregation.

Of course, an openended commitment to covenant discipleship does not imply lifetime membership in the same group. This will rarely be possible, given the nature of our mobile society today. People change jobs and homes, and schedules frequently change. But in joining a covenant discipleship group, people are making a commitment to change the pattern of their walk with Christ. They are making a transition to an accountable discipleship; and by definition, this means a permanent change in their Christian priorities and lifestyle.

When this is made clear at the outset, there are obviously a number of persons who hesitate and, in some instances, decide that this is not a commitment they wish to make at this point in their Christian pilgrimage. Most people considering covenant discipleship, however, find it a very affirming word that locks them into their decision and their calling. It also means that the attrition from covenant discipleship is quite minimal, and certainly much lower than from other forms of small group activity in congregations.

PILOT GROUPS

By far the most effective way of introducing covenant discipleship groups to a congregation is through pilot groups. These meet for at least a year, testing the format and preparing the congregation for the time when the groups are opened to the whole congregation.

There are a number of reasons why pilot groups have proved effective, but the most important is that they allow the congregation to consider with care the impact covenant discipleship will have on its life and work. Just as Jesus cautioned individuals against an impulsive commitment to discipleship (Mt. 20:1-16; Mk. 10:28-31; Lk. 13:22-30; 14:26-27; Jn. 13:1-17), so it must be made clear that covenant discipleship groups, albeit involving only some of the members, will open up a whole new understanding of Christian discipleship for the congregation as a whole, and mark an important step forward in its ministry and mission. Covenant discipleship groups will be role models in discipleship, and should be seen as a leadership-oriented activity.

"EXPLORATORY," NOT "EXPERIMENTAL"

The word *pilot* is important in this regard, because it does not mean "experimental." Pilot groups are not trying out covenant discipleship to see if it is worthwhile, any more than Jesus invited Simon, Andrew, James, and John to follow him for a trial period. Rather, pilot groups take the lead in exploring covenant discipleship on behalf of the congregation. They find out about covenant discipleship in the best possible way—by taking the first step in actually doing it. They use the same guidelines that will apply later when the groups are opened up to the entire membership of the church, and they establish many of the procedures that will integrate the groups later with the congregation.

PRACTICAL ADVANTAGES OF PILOT GROUPS

There are some further practical advantages to starting covenant discipleship with pilot groups:

- Pilot groups are a good preparation for introducing covenant discipleship to the congregation, in that they provide a source of leadership and expertise when the groups are introduced on a wider basis.

- Pilot groups can raise people's awareness of the concept of covenant discipleship. During the pilot year, word can be spread through the congregation. Questions can be raised and answered, so that the membership at large has a heightened expectancy when the groups are opened to everyone.

- Pilot groups do not place an undue administrative burden on the pastor and the church staff. Between the formation of a pilot group and the opening of the groups to the rest of the congregation, there is ample time to prepare for the logistics of wider participation.

- Pilot groups are able to explore covenant discipleship on behalf of the congregation without the pressure of success or failure. There are some hidden snags in the format of the groups, and it is helpful to have the freedom to encounter high and low points as an exploratory exercise.

- Questions and objections are best handled during the pilot process. The most common of these are dealt with in the next chapter, and they occur with marked regularity. Pilot groups allow ample time for questions to surface, and thus to forestall any widespread objections when the groups are opened to the congregation as a whole.

THE NUMBER OF PILOT GROUPS

The number of pilot groups depends very much on the size of the congregation. In most instances, one pilot group will suffice. But in larger congregations, and especially where there is a multiple staff, two or even three pilot groups may prove feasible. Experience has shown, however, that there should be no more than three pilot groups; otherwise they tend to assume more than a pilot role. They then become the sort of administrative burden they are designed to avoid, and it becomes difficult to nurture them through the procedures and the pitfalls of a pilot process.

PARTICIPATION OF THE PASTORAL STAFF

As we have already noted, it is very important that the pastoral staff of the congregation take part in the pilot group(s). In most congregations, where there will be only one pilot group, the pastor should be a member. In larger churches, associate staff should be assigned to second and third pilot groups.

The purpose of having staff persons in each group is not to provide permanent leadership, even though they will probably serve in this capacity during the first few weeks, contributing some basic skills in group dynamics. Thereafter, the role of leader rotates during the weekly meetings, giving each member a share in this responsibility, and also affording an opportunity for each member to share fully in the process of accountability. The importance of having the pastor take part in the pilot groups is rather to emphasize that covenant discipleship is *integral* to the life and work of the church. This is where the basics of discipleship are practiced, and thus where discipleship is role-modeled for the congregation.

PASTORAL INTEGRITY IN THE GROUP

Contrary to what many pastors fear, taking part in a covenant discipleship group in no way compromises their pastoral role in the congregation. The sharing tends to focus on how the members are living out their Christian discipleship in the world, and the content of each meeting is quite objective, focusing much more on what people have done than on what they have experienced. In the doing of discipleship, the basics are the same for all Christians, clergy or laity; and pastors need to be accountable for these basics no less than anyone else.

Interestingly, once pastors do take part in such a process of accountability, they and the other group members find a new understanding of one another. It becomes clear that the most natural support group for a pastor is not other pastors, but the pastor's own people. On the one hand, in the relatively short space of one hour and with the clear agenda of an agreed covenant, there is little risk of entering into deeper sharing which might encroach on issues of pastoral confidence. On the other hand, there is plenty of opportunity to sense the common journey pastor and people share together, and this mutual discovery is almost always an occasion of heightened affection and deepened understanding.

RECRUITMENT OF PILOT GROUPS

One of the most heartening aspects of implementing covenant discipleship groups is to find how many church members have been waiting for something like this to be offered. It is very rare indeed for a congregation not to have a cadre of members willing to make themselves accountable for their discipleship.

The recruitment of the pilot groups can thus be very matter-of-fact: announcements from the pulpit, in the worship bulletin, or in the church newsletter. In most instances, with copies of the covenant discipleship brochure also made available (order no. M299L), such an announcement will produce enough response to form at least one pilot group. If this does not happen, then clearly a more intentional invitation must be made. The pastor can make a direct approach to those members of the congregation who have shown their willingness over the years to engage in active Christian witness and service. An approach can likewise be made to those members who are searching for a deeper understanding of their faith.

Another way of extending a more intentional invitation is to arrange for presentations to various groups in the congregation—Sunday school classes or continuing education events. The video set *Discovering the Modern Methodists* (order no. M301VC) can be helpful in this regard. Alternatively, the covenant discipleship office in Nashville will be pleased to make recommendations from a roster of trained consultants. Whichever method is used, most congregations will have at least a few members ready for the sort of commitment afforded by covenant discipleship. When they are informed about it, and sense that the pastor is willing to make it a full component of the ministry and mission of the church, they will respond.

SOME ADDITIONAL "NUTS AND BOLTS"

Occasionally a congregation may find that there are too many volunteers for the maximum of three pilot groups. If this happens, it is strongly recommended not to form a fourth pilot group, for the reasons already given. A request can always be made for volunteers to withdraw from the pilot process, and to wait until the following year when the groups will be opened to the whole congregation.

By the same token, while a pilot group can remain open to new members during the first month of its meetings, it should be closed for the remainder of the pilot year. Changes in membership tend to be disruptive for groups involved in something new, and they should be allowed the freedom to concentrate on their task. If there are persons with an especially high level of interest who were not able to join a pilot group during its first month, their interest can be sustained by involving them in preparations for the weekend when the groups are opened to the entire congregation.

In all other respects, pilot groups function just like every other covenant discipleship group. Indeed, as "pilot" groups, they are doing what other groups will do in a year's time. Pilot group members should therefore get to know the companion volume, *Covenant Discipleship,* in some detail. They should follow its recommendations, and delve into the Wesleyan tradition of class meetings outlined in the opening chapters of the volume. They should also feel free to exercise a degree of flexibility in their meetings, since they are the first in the congregation to be exploring these guidelines and procedures.

At no time, however, should they lose sight of their role as pilot groups. Others in the congregation will be ready in a year or so to benefit from their expertise as they form additional groups. When that time comes, the experience and the testimonial of the pilot group members will be of vital importance.

RELATING PILOT GROUPS TO THE CONGREGATION

An important dimension of the pilot process is letting the other church members know that covenant discipleship is being explored with a view to incorporating it into the total ministry and mission of the congregation. This means that members of the pilot group(s) should make every effort to talk to others about what is happening in their meetings. Confidentiality should be protected, of course, but there is much that can be shared in a number of ways with the membership as a whole:

- *Sunday School Classes.* Members of pilot groups can offer to make a presentation, handing out literature on covenant discipleship and answering the questions that people always have when something concerns their discipleship.

- *Sunday Morning Worship.* A brief word of testimony from a pilot group member can be very effective during the time allocated for announcements and the sharing of congregational concerns.

- *Church Organizations.* Opportunities abound for sharing information with the Administrative Board or Council, United Methodist Women, United Methodist Men, United Methodist Youth Fellowship, and others.

LENGTH OF THE PILOT PROCESS

The recommended span for the pilot process in covenant discipleship is one year. This is not rigid, of course. Sometimes the pastor and the group will sense a readiness among the members that requires the date to be brought forward. In most instances, however, a year will be needed for pilot groups to do their work thoroughly. This allows them to experience the growing sense of grace which binds a covenant discipleship group together in its obedience to Jesus Christ. It also allows them to experience and grow through some of the difficulties encountered in the discipline of accountability. To use "muscle" of the church which has not been activated for some time will probably mean some aches and pains until it is in shape, and it usually takes a year for this to happen.

Most important of all, a year's experience enables the members of pilot groups to provide sure guidance to the new groups when they are formed. Covenant discipleship cannot be effective if it is planted in shallow ground. It must be planted deep for a rich harvest of discipleship—and seeds planted deep always take longer to germinate.

OPENING THE GROUPS TO THE CONGREGATION

Pilot groups should begin with the clear objective of opening covenant discipleship to the whole congregation approximately one year later. This will take the form of a special covenant discipleship weekend, and a date should be placed on the church calendar, with publicity arranged well in advance.

The extension of the groups to the whole membership is a critical transition for the congregation. A number of members will form new covenant discipleship groups, taking a step forward in their discipleship that they have probably been contemplating for some time. But it will also be the birthing of a new understanding of discipleship throughout the congregation; and, as with all births, there will be a degree of unpredictability about it. The pilot group members should therefore be watchful as well as ready in preparing for this culmination of their work.

THE COVENANT DISCIPLESHIP WEEKEND

The covenant discipleship weekend is the proven way of opening covenant discipleship groups to the congregation as a whole. As we have already noted, by no means will everyone be ready to join a group; but it is vitally important that everyone be *invited* to join. In this way, the congregation as a whole can have a sense of ownership of this new dimension to their ministry and mission. Likewise, those who make the commitment to join a group can be affirmed in their decision, without the rest of the membership feeling that covenant discipleship is in any way exclusive.

SCHEDULING THE WEEKEND

Many congregations have found early spring or early fall to be a good time to schedule a covenant discipleship weekend. There is, however, only one sure guideline in determining the date, and that is the point at which the pilot members feel they have come to understand the nature and purpose of covenant discipleship, and can confidently share it with everyone else in the congregation.

INVITING A GUEST LEADER OR PREACHER

The advantages of having an outside leader and preacher for the weekend are the same as for any special event: fresh insights and perspectives, affirmation of covenant discipleship from an independent source, and freedom for the pastor and pilot groups members to provide support as full participants. In addition, leading a covenant discipleship weekend requires a sensitive understanding of the groups and the ability to preach a direct invitational sermon. The covenant discipleship office in Nashville can recommend a number of clergy and laity who have been specially trained for this work.

On the other hand, there is usually no one better qualified to preach at and lead the weekend than the pastor of the congregation and the pilot group members. They will have worked together in covenant discipleship for at least a year, and will be sensitive to the readiness of the congregation for this new commitment. Thus, while a guest leader and preacher can often enhance a weekend, there are very few instances where such a person is absolutely necessary.

PREPARING THE PILOT GROUP MEMBERS

We have already stressed how important the pilot group members are for the introduction of covenant discipleship, and their participation in this weekend is no less significant. Their testimony to what has been happening during the pilot year is one of the most effective aspects of the event, and their role in helping new groups to get started is indispensable. Well in advance, therefore, the pilot group members should be prepared for the part they will play in the weekend.

First, they should be ready to give an account of their pilot group experience. There are formal occasions during the weekend when they will be called upon to do so, and there are likely to be a number of informal occasions as well. This is not to say that their testimonies should be over-prepared: spontaneity will be their most winsome quality. But it may be a good idea to have a practice session ahead of time. Many people today are hesitant to give personal testimonies, and a "dry run" can often help to overcome apprehension. They should also be encouraged to be quite candid in what they say. As pilot members, they have been leading the way for the congregation, and they should not conceal the difficulties of covenant discipleship any more than they should downplay the advantages.

HELPING TO START NEW GROUPS

With regard to their helping to start new groups, a question often asked by pilot group members is whether they have to disband their existing groups and divide themselves among the new ones. It is a question with an interesting track record in covenant discipleship, and there is no short answer.

When the pilot process was first introduced as the most effective way of implementing covenant discipleship groups in a congregation, it was strongly recommended that the pilot members should divide among the new groups following the weekend. This recommendation quickly encountered resistance, however, as pilot groups found they had come to experience a oneness in Christ they did not wish to lose. As a result, a compromise procedure was suggested. If a pilot group did not wish to disband after the covenant discipleship weekend, the members were asked instead to give an hour each week to provide leadership for a new group during its formative stages, in addition to meeting with their own groups. Once the new groups had found their feet, the pilot members could withdraw, and revert to just meeting with their own group—which by then, of course, had become one of a number of covenant discipleship groups in the congregation.

Subsequently, however, there have been reports from congregations on both procedures; and without exception, where pilot groups disbanded and divided themselves among new groups, the results were much more positive than where the pilot group members merely agreed to "do overtime" for a few weeks. Those who adopted the compromise suggestion wished they had resisted the appeal of staying together.

The answer to the question of whether or not pilot groups should disband is therefore a qualified affirmative. Yes, they should disband—except in instances where this meets such stiff resistance that it would prove detrimental to the groups as a whole.

MATERIALS AND PUBLICITY

As a final preparation for the weekend, there should be a good supply of covenant discipleship materials on hand. These are listed at the end of this volume, with instructions for ordering. The weekend will generate a high level of interest in covenant discipleship, and the resources will be useful not only for those who join groups, but also for the congregation as a whole.

The weekend should also be intensively publicized in the life and work of the congregation. However well the pilot group members have done their work in this area, the event must be intentionally promoted as a critical turning point in the life of the congregation. To regard it merely as another programmatic offering will be self-defeating. It is nothing less than the launching of a whole new generation of leaders in discipleship, and it must therefore be given appropriate emphasis.

THE FORMAT OF THE WEEKEND

The following paragraphs describe the format for a covenant discipleship weekend that has been effective in a wide range of congregations for more than a decade. It should be stressed, however, that covenant discipleship groups are designed to develop leadership *in congregations;* and insofar as each congregation has distinctive characteristics and traditions, the format should be considered adaptable to different contexts. The purpose of the weekend is to extend the invitation to all of the congregation to join a covenant discipleship group. Whatever is most effective in reaching the membership as a whole should therefore govern the shape and the planning of the event.

THE FRIDAY EVENING MEAL

On the Friday evening, it is a good idea to begin with a church-wide meeting—if practicable, a covered dish supper or a family evening with dessert or refreshments. After the meal, the pastor or the guest speaker may give an introduction to the concept of covenant discipleship, following which the pilot group members can talk about their experiences of the past year. Their testimonies are invariably a high moment in the weekend.

This is also a good time for any lingering doubts or objections to be aired. A time of dialogue should follow, with the speaker and the pilot group members forming a panel to answer questions from the floor. As the discussion unfolds, it quickly becomes clear how the pilot group members have been breaking the new ground of covenant discipleship on behalf of the congregation. It is reassuring for everyone to hear that joining a group is a response to God's call, and not something that is expected of everyone in the church.

If there is a guest speaker for the weekend, he or she will need to meet the pilot members beforehand, and agree how to divide the time available for the evening. It is best if the presentations and panel discussion can be kept to one hour, or ninety minutes at most. The objective is simple: to leave with the audience a clear picture of what a covenant discipleship group is, and what is involved in joining one.

THE SATURDAY SEMINAR AND ROLE PLAY

On the Saturday, preferably in the morning, a training seminar may be held. This should have two sessions: first, an account of the theology behind covenant discipleship groups, along with something of their origin in the Methodist tradition; and second, a practical explanation of how a covenant discipleship group functions, with members of the pilot group inviting other participants in the seminar to join them in performing a short role play of a typical weekly meeting.

The value of this role play cannot be overemphasized. It does not have to go through the whole of a covenant, but it should include a sample clause from each of the four areas of the General Rule of Discipleship: compassion, justice, worship, and devotion. It should also include the other procedures of a weekly group meeting described in the handbook, *Covenant Discipleship:* an opening prayer and reading of the covenant, concluding prayer concerns, appointment of the leader for the next week, any personal clauses, and any actions the group has agreed to take with regard to the covenant. Afterwards, the seminar participants should be asked to reflect on what has happened in dialogue with the role players—a discussion which often raises the most meaningful questions of the entire morning.

The role play shows more convincingly than anything else that covenant discipleship groups are not at all threatening, but are rather an assurance of comradeship on a common journey. It also provides a clear demonstration of mutual accountability in forging a faithful discipleship. Since other persons from the seminar are invited to join the pilot group members in playing these roles, there is no opportunity to rehearse; and thus there is almost always a spontaneous outpouring of relief and delight as the role play proceeds. It reveals a mutual concern for everyone's discipleship, and a mutual need to be in company with those of like mind and spirit; and it reveals, albeit in a training context, that the Christian journey is not solitary—that there are indeed trustworthy companions along the way.

RESOURCES FOR THE SEMINAR

If there is a guest speaker for the weekend, the seminar will, of course, be his or her responsibility. If not, a good way to begin the Saturday morning is with one or more parts of the video set *Discovering the Modern Methodists* (order no. M301VC). This consists of four twenty-minute presentations, with an accompanying study guide. Used with the companion volume, *Covenant Discipleship,* and drawing on other resources such as *The Early Methodist Class Meeting* (order no. DR017B) for additional detail and content, the pastor and the pilot group members can provide a well-informed seminar for interested persons in the congregation.

The purpose of the seminar is to provide a more detailed introduction to covenant discipleship than is possible on the Friday evening. At the same time, it allows the pilot members to interact with persons who are likely to become the nucleus of the new covenant discipleship groups in the congregation. There should therefore be a warm collegiality extended by the pastor and the pilot group members. This can be affirmed at the conclusion of the morning by asking for their assistance when the invitation is extended during Sunday morning worship (see p. 84). It helps considerably to have a good initial response to this; and if those who intend to join a new group will come forward promptly to make their commitment along with the pilot group members, it will encourage others to follow.

THE SATURDAY EVENING

When there is a guest speaker for the weekend, it is helpful to schedule a Saturday evening meeting with the administrative leadership of the congregation. The purpose of this is not to recruit them for group membership, but rather to ask for their support in accepting covenant discipleship as a new dimension of the ministry and mission of the congregation. The integration of the groups into the life and work of the church is vital to their purpose and effectiveness, and such a meeting can greatly facilitate that process.

If there is no guest speaker, this support can be sought at regular administrative meetings prior to the weekend. Even so, such a meeting can still be helpful, to make sure that there are no misunderstandings about covenant discipleship or its place in the leadership of the congregation.

THE SUNDAY WORSHIP SERVICE

On Sunday morning, the weekend comes to its climax in the worship service, at which the invitation is made to the entire congregation to join a covenant discipleship group. The order of worship should indicate clearly that the focus of the service is to call persons to enter into a mutual accountability for their discipleship. The hymns should center on service and obedience to the will of God, and the text for the sermon should reflect the theme of working out our salvation—Matthew 21:28-32, for example, or Philippians 2:12-13.

There should also be a clear indication that there will be an invitation following the sermon to make a public commitment to a covenant discipleship group. This can be done by including in the bulletin a sample covenant of discipleship such as the one on p. 85.

THE INVITATION TO JOIN A GROUP

The invitation to join a covenant discipleship group is the most important moment of the weekend, and it should be extended without any pressure or manipulation. Covenant discipleship is very much a vocational activity, and those who are ready will make their commitment in response to the Holy Spirit. All they need is a simple, straightforward invitation. At the same time, it should be made clear that those who respond are making their commitment as part of the church's ministry and mission. They are being asked to come forward as a public act of dedication so that the congregation as a whole can affirm them in their decision and support them in their weekly disciplines.

The liturgy, the music, the scripture readings, and the prayers can all assist in preparing for this moment. But there should also be some place in the service for a brief description of covenant discipleship: what is involved in joining a group, and how the weekly meetings are conducted. At this point the sample covenant in the bulletin insert can be used to demonstrate that there is nothing unusual about a covenant of discipleship. The difference is that members of a covenant discipleship group agree to be accountable for *keeping* it.

The preacher should also explain beforehand how the invitation to join a covenant discipleship group will be extended at the close

A SAMPLE COVENANT OF DISCIPLESHIP

Knowing that Jesus Christ died that I might have eternal life, I herewith pledge myself to be his disciple, witnessing to his saving grace, and seeking to follow his teachings under the guidance of the Holy Spirit. I faithfully pledge my time, my skills, my resources, and my strength to search out God's will for me, and to obey.

I will worship each Sunday unless prevented.

*I will receive the sacrament of Holy
Communion each week.*

*I will pray each day, privately,
and with my family or with friends.*

I will read and study the scriptures each day.

I will return to Christ the first tenth of all I receive.

*I will spend four hours each month to further
the cause of the disadvantaged in my community.*

*When I am aware of injustice to others,
I will not remain silent.*

*I will obey the promptings of the Holy Spirit
to serve God and my neighbor.*

*I will heed the warnings of the Holy Spirit
not to sin against God and my neighbor.*

*I will prayerfully care for my body
and for the world in which I live.*

I hereby make my commitment, trusting in the grace of God to give me the will and the strength to keep this covenant.

Date: _____ Signed: _____

of the sermon. This helps to reduce any tensions people may have about pulpiteering techniques. In addition, it provides an openness and sensitivity to the work of the Holy Spirit in their hearts during the preaching of the Word.

At the conclusion of the sermon, the invitation to join a covenant discipleship group should be extended to everyone. Those who wish to respond should come forward and stand at the front of the sanctuary. The organist should be ready to play quietly while people are responding. It is not helpful to have a heavy silence at this juncture, nor is it a good idea to have people respond during the singing of a hymn. People need time to make their decision prayerfully, and it may take several minutes for everyone to come forward from different places in the sanctuary. The background music should therefore continue until all movement has ceased.

THE PRAYER OF COMMITMENT

The guest preacher or the pastor should then lead those who have come forward in a prayer of commitment, such as the following from Wesley's *Covenant Service:*

> *I am no longer my own, but thine.*
> *Put me to what thou wilt, rank me with whom thou wilt;*
> *put me to doing, put me to suffering;*
> *let me be employed for thee or laid aside for thee,*
> *exalted for thee or trodden under foot for thee;*
> *let me be full, let me be empty;*
> *let me have all things, let me have nothing;*
> *I freely and heartily yield all things*
> *to thy pleasure and disposal.*
> *And now, O glorious and blessed God,*
> *Father, Son and Holy Spirit,*
> *thou art mine, and I am thine.*
> *So be it.*
> *And the covenant which I have made on earth,*
> *let it be ratified in heaven. Amen.*

Following this prayer, the preacher should thank the people for making their commitment, and inform them that there will be a short meeting following the service at which the new covenant discipleship groups will be formed. If there are any who cannot stay behind, they should be asked to sign the sample covenant in their bulletin, and leave it with an usher or at the church office, so that they can be contacted during the following week.

AN OPEN INVITATION

The preacher should also announce to the congregation that if there are any who did not feel able to come forward to make their commitment in this way, they are still welcome at the meeting after the service. Furthermore, the covenant discipleship groups are now open to everyone to join at any time. There are no conditions for joining other than a willingness to commit to the weekly meeting, and an intent to follow the clauses of the group covenant.

The people should then be asked to return to their seats, and worship should continue with the remainder of the service. This symbolic re-uniting of the people with the congregation further ensures that the whole body affirms the decision of these members to join covenant discipleship groups, and that the groups are a fully recognized dimension of the congregation's ministry and mission.

The next step is to translate all of this into the reality of new covenant discipleship groups, and we will explain how that is done in Chapter 5.

Chapter Five

Organizing Covenant Discipleship Groups

FORMING THE NEW GROUPS

Following the covenant discipleship weekend, the organization of new groups should be implemented as soon as possible. The best time for this is straight after the Sunday morning worship service at which the invitation is extended to the congregation, since the procedures usually take no more than thirty minutes. People are willing to stay for this short time rather than come to a meeting at another time; and they are also ready to act on the commitment they have just made in the worship service. Not everyone who made the commitment to join a group will be there, but there should be enough in attendance to draw up a tentative schedule of dates and times for the new groups.

If a meeting straight after the worship service is not possible, it can be held in the afternoon or evening of the Sunday, or later that week. It should not be delayed for more than a week, however, since this loses the momentum of the weekend, and almost always results in a lower attendance—or worse, in the loss of some of those who made a commitment.

THE ORGANIZATIONAL MEETING

Because of the nature and dynamic of covenant discipleship groups, it matters less than in other types of small groups whether the members are compatible. Still, it is helpful to avoid unnecessary conflicts of personality, and the following method of organizing the groups has been found to work easily and effectively.

The follow-up meeting should be held in a large room, with sheets of newsprint posted around the walls. Once everyone is assembled, the guest speaker or the pastor should give a brief introduction to covenant discipleship for those who were not at the Friday or Saturday sessions of the weekend. The nature and purpose of the groups can be re-stated, and any further questions addressed.

CONDITIONS OF GROUP MEMBERSHIP

The most common questions during the follow-up meeting tend to focus on whether there are any conditions or restrictions concerning membership in a covenant discipleship group. These issues are addressed in detail in the companion volume, *Covenant Discipleship,* but they can be summed up very simply: Covenant discipleship groups function without any membership restrictions concerning age, sex, or marital status.

For logistical reasons it may be that a group is made up of men or women only. But the great majority of groups are mixed, since the task of discipleship applies to all persons alike. Some married couples, for example, prefer to join the same group; others prefer to be in separate groups. Some families wish to be in a group together; in other instances, young people prefer to be in a covenant group apart from their parents. There are no hard and fast rules.

INTERGENERATIONAL GROUPS

There is one important advantage to having intergenerational groups, whether or not they comprise members of the same family. For a young person to take part in a weekly meeting where adults are holding themselves accountable for their Christian discipleship is a profoundly formative experience. Indeed, the perceived lack of such accountability among adults today is a significant factor in the loss of many young people from the ranks of committed discipleship in the church. If a young person wishes to be part of an intergenerational group, therefore, this should in no way be discouraged. Older persons do not need to feel embarrassed about being accountable to younger persons, nor should younger persons feel awkward about doing the same. Nothing could be more wholesome for both.

COVENANT DISCIPLESHIP FOR YOUNG PEOPLE

There are particular settings, however, where young people need to join a group with their peers, and they should certainly not be discouraged from doing so. Indeed, there are two adaptations of covenant discipleship to meet these needs: for young people in congregations; and for students on college campuses. The resources are: *Branch Groups: Covenant Discipleship for Youth,* by Lisa Grant (order no. DR067B); and *Covenants on Campus: Covenant Discipleship Groups for College and University Students* (order no. DR099B), by Kim A. Hauenstein-Mallet and Kenda Creasy Dean. Details of these and other covenant discipleship resources can be found at the end of this volume.

DAYS AND TIMES

Since the only conditions for membership in a covenant discipleship group are the commitment to be there and the willingness to be accountable for the covenant which the group itself writes, the only question to be asked of a prospective member is, Can you make this day and time a priority in your weekly schedule? By the same token, the only question a prospective member needs to ask about a covenant discipleship group is, What day and time does it meet? The next step in the follow-up meeting is therefore to ask people to suggest some days and times convenient for them to meet. As these are called out, they should be written up on separate sheets of newsprint, until all possible times and days are prominently on display.

Everyone in the room should then be asked to sign up for the group most convenient for them. This permits a great degree of movement and flexibility, during the course of which people can select not only the best day and time, but also any preferred companions without giving the appearance of rejecting any person or any group. It is also helpful if everyone adds her or his address and telephone number to the sheet. This saves a great deal of time and effort in the collation of the group lists afterwards.

THE SIZE OF A GROUP

The recommended maximum size of a group is seven, and the only reason for this is logistics. If a group is to be held accountable for a covenant which may have ten or more clauses, it is difficult to involve more than seven people in a question-and-answer session lasting only one hour. And since the one strict rule of covenant discipleship is to finish exactly on the hour, the size of the group must be limited accordingly.

On the other hand, there is no minimum number for a group. A few groups have worked very effectively with three, or even two members. Though by and large, when groups have fewer than four members, the dynamic of the meeting is more difficult. Absences are felt more acutely and there is less diversity of Christian discipleship. In practice, the average covenant discipleship group numbers five or six, leaving room for new members to join, yet also leaving a good group on those occasions when not everyone can be present.

If a sizeable number of the group have work which frequently takes them out of town, membership may be extended to eight or nine, with the expectancy that there will always be one or two absent. Again, there are no hard and fast rules. Nor is there any limit to the number of groups meeting at the same time. If twelve people sign up for a particular day and time, then two groups should be formed. In larger congregations, there are often multiple group meetings scheduled at the more popular times—Sunday afternoon, for example, or Wednesday evening.

LOCATIONS AND CONVENERS

When everyone has signed up for a group, two further steps should be taken. First, each group should agree on where it will hold its first meeting. There is no rule for where this should be. A few groups decide to meet in homes; most decide to meet in a room at the church. The only proviso is that the meeting place should be private, comfortable, and conducive to the purpose of the group. Large classrooms, for example, should be avoided.

Second, each group should designate one of its members as convener. Conveners are not the same as group leaders. The leader of a covenant discipleship group is merely the member who acts as questioner during the weekly meeting, asking the members to give an account of their discipleship in light of the group covenant. Moreover, the role of leader rotates week by week, so that everyone shares the responsibility. Conveners, on the other hand, are "contact persons" for the group, liaising with the church staff, and making sure that housekeeping matters are dealt with on a regular basis. It is best if they are appointed on a yearly basis.

All of this organizational business for the groups can be accomplished in a relatively short time, and the meeting can then be adjourned. During the next week, however, there is a great deal of work to be done by the church office, and also by the pilot group members, whose role is pivotal in the successful launching of the new groups.

COLLATING THE GROUP INFORMATION

At the conclusion of the organizational meeting, someone should accept responsibility for gathering all the information: the sign-up sheets with names and addresses of the new members; the group conveners and meeting locations; and the bulletin inserts that were handed in after the worship service, since they will include the names of persons who were not able to attend the follow-up meeting.

All of this information should then be collated. If a congregation is large enough to have a paid office staff, this should be made a priority for the coming week. Where there is no paid staff, pilot group members should accept the responsibility. A list should be made of all the new groups, indicating the members, the conveners, and the days and times of their meetings, and circulated during the next week to everyone who has made a commitment to join a group.

With the list there should be a circular letter, inviting those who could not attend the organizational meeting to select a group, and offering an opportunity to those who have already opted for a group to make a change if they wish. It should announce when the groups will start meeting, and give a time by which group selections should be completed.

The mailing should also include a copy of the *Christian Formation Brochure* (order no. M299L). This provides an overview of covenant discipleship, describing the nature and purpose of the groups, and listing the various resources for new group members.

THE ROLE OF THE PILOT GROUP MEMBERS

The pilot group members now face what is perhaps their most important task: helping the new groups to get started. The advantages of having pilot groups disband and the members assigned permanently to new groups have already been discussed (above, p. 80). But some pilot groups will prefer to continue as they are; in which case, the members should be asked to help new groups to get started while continuing to meet with their own groups.

The following guidelines may be used or adapted by pilot group members as they implement this critical transition. The pilot members should also be familiar with the relevant sections of the companion volume, *Covenant Discipleship.*

GUIDELINES FOR PILOT GROUP MEMBERS WORKING WITH NEW COVENANT DISCIPLESHIP GROUPS

1. *Establish contact with the convener of your new group as soon as possible.*

Introduce yourself to the convener, and be as supportive and encouraging as you can, letting him or her know that you are going to be part of the group, or that you will be attending their meetings for the first few weeks to help them get started.

2. *Check the date, time, and place of the first meeting.*

Ask the convener to make sure that everyone in the group knows these details. The convener should also check that everyone has received the circular letter and the membership list.

3. *Take a supply of covenant discipleship materials to the first meeting.*

Consult with the church office beforehand to see whether items are available on consignment or can be offered at reduced cost. Take to the first meeting a supply of the handbook, *Covenant Discipleship,* the *Covenant Discipleship Quarterly,* and the *Covenant Discipleship Journal,* along with order blanks for the entire range of covenant discipleship materials. Be ready to advise new members on which items they will find especially helpful. Stress the importance of each person having a copy of the handbook and also subscribing to the *Quarterly.*

4. *Assume the role of leader at the first meeting.*

Even though the role of leader will rotate in due course, it will be best if you assume it for the first few weeks. At the initial meeting, ask members to introduce themselves, and try to establish a very informal atmosphere. Walk people through the handbook, pointing out the discussion questions at the end of the opening chapters, and showing how the practical aspects of the groups are laid out in detail. Spend the rest of the hour describing what your covenant discipleship group has meant to you, and answering any questions.

At the end of the meeting, be sure that the following points are covered:

• Agree on the time and place of next week's meeting.
• Make sure that someone will contact any absent members.

- Announce that next week the group will begin to write its covenant, and that members should look at the sample covenant in the handbook to see what is involved.
- Suggest that members also begin reading the rest of the handbook, and be ready to consider the first set of discussion questions.

5. *At the next meeting, again assume the role of leader.*

Continue as leader the following week, and after the usual opening prayer take the first half hour for discussion questions from the handbook. During the second half hour, start writing the covenant. Begin with the sample covenant in the handbook, but stress that this is only a starting point. The group members should be clear that this will be *their* covenant, and they should not include anything they themselves are not ready to attempt.

Pace the meeting so that members always feel at ease about asking questions. Keep everyone's interest, but not at the expense of anyone's involvement in the process.

6. *Follow the same format for the next three or four meetings.*

For the next three or four meetings, spend the first half hour with discussion questions from the handbook, and the second half hour in refining the group covenant until it is agreed and written. Then spend the second half hour introducing the process of accountability.

Be flexible with this timetable. If you feel that the group is ready to move into a full hour of accountability, there is no need to continue with the half hour of discussion. But if there are still some unanswered questions, then carry on with the discussion period each week until they are answered. Your aim should be to have the group ready to begin its full process of covenant accountability by the end of six weeks.

7. *Hand over the leadership at the seventh meeting.*

Unless there are serious problems with the group, you should aim to hand over the leadership by the seventh week. If you are a permanent member of the group, this is the time to start rotating the weekly leadership. If your pilot group has decided to stay together and you are acting only as adviser to the new group, this is the time to withdraw, letting the group know that you are always available for consultation. Also let them know that there will be regular quarterly meetings when problems and questions can be raised (below, p. 106).

FOLLOW-UP MEETING WITH PILOT MEMBERS

It is advisable to schedule a session with the pilot members one month after the groups have begun to meet. This accomplishes several things:

- It surfaces any difficulties which the groups might be experiencing. Many of these will be common problems, which can often be resolved by mutual advice.

- It provides a means of sharing fresh ideas. The formation of the groups is always an exciting time, generating a great deal of enthusiasm, and fostering a context for new ideas and new promptings of the Holy Spirit.

- It continues the process of leadership development which covenant discipleship is designed to foster. Remember, *covenant discipleship groups are not for persons, but for congregations.* The pilot group members are the first to experience this directly, and their expertise should be used to the full.

"ACHES AND PAINS"

Once the groups have been organized and have begun to meet each week, additional questions are likely to emerge which go beyond mere logistics. John Wesley described the early class meetings as the sinews of the early Methodist movement, and as we noted in the previous chapter, there is the same need today to use the muscle of the church. Muscle is not the whole body; but if it is neglected, what ought to be healthy growth can easily become excess fat, draining the pastoral resources of a congregation.

By contrast, when there is well-tuned muscle, the body is strong, lean, and active. This is what begins to happen when covenant discipleship groups allow committed Christians to exercise accountability for their walk with Christ. There is, however, an initial drawback to this newfound health and strength. As with all muscle that has not been used for some time, there are "aches and pains," not only among the members of the groups, but among the congregation as a whole. The living out of the General Rule of Discipleship by the groups will not always be agreeable to everyone, even though in the long term their leadership will equip the church for a discipleship which is resilient, faithful, and challenging.

DEALING WITH OBJECTIONS

These aches and pains become unavoidable when the challenge of accountable discipleship impacts other members of the congregation through the weekly witness of the covenant discipleship groups. As with all of God's gracious initiatives, this occasions resistance, usually in the form of objections to covenant discipleship. Some of the individual objections are dealt with in the companion volume, *Covenant Discipleship*. The following are more likely to occur in a congregational setting.

Objection

> *Covenant discipleship groups imply an elitism*
> *in the Christian life.*

There are those who feel that when people gather into small groups for intentional discipleship, whether through acts of compassion, justice, worship, or devotion, a distinction is implied between themselves and everyone else in the church. The only inference to draw from such a distinction is that these persons regard themselves as superior.

Answer

The answer is that members of covenant discipleship groups, far from implying a superiority, spiritual or otherwise, are declaring to each other and to the body of the church that, if anything, they are *in*ferior. They are unable to sustain their discipleship on their own. They need the help and support of others, even for the basics of Christian living. If this is a superiority, then it is a superiority of need.

The closest parallels to covenant discipleship groups in contemporary society are organizations such as Alcoholics Anonymous and Weight Watchers, where a common weakness is confessed and dealt with through the help of others who have the same problem. Members of covenant discipleship groups likewise confess a common weakness: their inability to be obedient disciples of Jesus Christ. Even though they are forgiven and reconciled sinners, there remains what the Wesleys described as "inbred sin"—that residual old nature which still resists the gracious initiatives of God. The mark of covenant discipleship members is not only their recognition of this tendency, but also their taking some common-sense steps to deal with it. They have come to see the importance of "watching over one another in love," and their sense is one of need, not superiority.

Objection

A written covenant is unnecessarily legalistic.

There are those who object to covenant discipleship groups on the grounds that a written covenant ties a person to unnecessary rules and regulations, and restricts the freedom of discipleship which is the mark of new life in Christ.

Answer

The issues behind this objection are dealt with in Chapter 1: the deceptive emphasis on personal faith in our Protestant tradition, reinforced today by a consumerist culture which teaches us to demand what we choose and reject what displeases us. This leads us into the pitfall of shaping Christian discipleship according to our preferences rather than to the teachings of Jesus.

On this premise, the answer to the objection lies in a comparison with the secular contracts which people honor in the midst of so much else that is inconsistent: credit card accounts, car payments, real estate agreements, and the like. Compared with the fickleness of so much Christian discipleship today, these contracts are relatively sacrosanct, contrasting markedly with Christians who are unwilling to make even a minimal commitment to the basics of their discipleship.

Objection

*Covenant discipleship groups deny the
power of the Holy Spirit.*

This objection tends to come from persons who have received the baptism of the Holy Spirit, or what is sometimes termed the *second blessing*. It stems from the strong conviction that the whole of Christian discipleship is an expression of grace, a free gift of the Holy Spirit. Any implication that our own efforts can sustain our discipleship is therefore tantamount to a denial of spiritual gifts. Indeed, an emphasis on the obligations of discipleship may well prevent us from expecting the power of the Holy Spirit; and what we do not expect, we are not likely to receive.

Answer

The answer to this objection is twofold. In the first place, covenant discipleship groups do not deny the freedom of the Holy Spirit. Rather, they acknowledge the true variety of God's spiritual gifts. Those whose spiritual gifts are sufficient to maintain an obedient discipleship without the practice of mutual accountability clearly have no need of such a group. But that does not deny the validity of covenant discipleship groups for those whose spiritual gifts are less effectual.

In the second place, participation in a covenant discipleship group can be a gracious way of sharing spiritual gifts with persons whose obedience comes more painstakingly. Besides this, to feel so secure in the presence and power of the Holy Spirit as to disdain a weekly check-up may indicate a spiritual pride that borders on humility—but is pride nonetheless.

Objection

A Fear of "Virtuoso Religiousness"

This objection has already been mentioned as the reason why some people hesitate to join a covenant discipleship group. It emerges even more strongly when the groups begin to meet, primarily as a feeling of inferiority on the part of those who perceive themselves as quite ordinary Christians, and therefore likely to be "shown up" by more "saintly" members. The most threatening figure in all of this is often the pastor, who is presumed to be well advanced in spiritual disciplines.

Answer

One of the most rewarding aspects of introducing covenant discipleship groups into a congregation is the tremendous relief expressed when these "ordinary" Christians find that the "saints" are just as ordinary as themselves. This is especially the case when the members of the pastor's group discover that she or he has just as much difficulty as anyone else in keeping to the General Rule of Discipleship. To find that one's pastor must struggle to maintain a devotional life, or to be faithful in standing firm for God's justice in the world, is a heartening discovery for the average church member. Not that this in any way demeans the standing of pastors. On the contrary, being identified as fellow pilgrims in the Christian life provides encouragement for those of their parishioners who lack confidence in their faith and their discipleship.

By the same token, members discover that spiritual perception is less important in a covenant discipleship group than what a person has accomplished week by week in following the teachings of Jesus; and the basics of Jesus' teachings prove to be very straight-forward. Those whose discipleship has been tempered through years of trial and error in learning obedience are the ones who emerge with true authority. Whereas those whose religious experience has perhaps obscured a brittle and uncertain Christian life, or those whose work for justice has perhaps concealed an avoidance of direct encounter with Christ, are brought to the essentials of their discipleship with new depths of insight.

Objection

A lifetime commitment to any kind of group
is impracticable and unrealistic.

Of all objections, this is perhaps the most honest. Given the nature of our society, the argument goes, few if any of us are in a position to make this sort of commitment. Rather than make a promise which will prove impossible to keep, would it not be more realistic to enter into a conditional covenant which stipulates a limited time? The group could always renew the covenant for a further period if desired. Besides which, the argument continues, a person's needs will change through a lifetime, and it is unlikely that a covenant discipleship group will prove consistently helpful.

Answer

This objection seems to be pragmatic, but frequently it is spiritual—the final resistance of a person who is close to a deeper walk with Christ, but has not yet decided to take the next step. It makes the protest disarmingly honest.

The first answer is to make clear that joining a covenant discipleship group is a commitment to mutual accountability as part of one's Christian lifestyle. It is not a commitment to one particular group. Of course people are going to move around, change employment, change homes, and change churches; and of course people will change throughout their Christian life and develop different needs. But covenant discipleship groups are a point of accountability for the General Rule of Discipleship, the very *basics* of Christian discipleship; and these basics do not change. If a covenant discipleship member has to change churches for any reason, therefore, the first step to be taken on joining the new congregation is to join another covenant discipleship group—or to start one.

The second answer brings us back to the question of common sense. *If* Jesus Christ is the way, the truth, and the life, and *if* there are well-tried ways of opening ourselves to the grace of the Holy Spirit, then the issue is not whether a lifetime commitment is practicable or realistic, but whether we can afford *not* to make it, given the basic obligations of our discipleship.

Objection

> *What is so different about covenant discipleship?*
> *Surely there are enough programs already.*

This objection stems from the multiplicity of programs and strategies being offered in the church today with precisely the same objectives as covenant discipleship: the revitalization of congregations and a return to faithful discipleship. Indeed, there is often a degree of frustration in local congregations over which of these many offerings to choose. Even when a congregation stays with denominational materials, the array is overwhelming. What is the difference, for example, between covenant discipleship groups and other small group models, such as *Disciple* Bible Study, or the reunion groups of *Walk to Emmaus*, or *Lay Witness*, or *Disciples Engaged*, or the *Experiment in Practical Christianity*, or the *John Wesley Great Experiment (Ten Brave Christians)?*[24]

Answer

This is not the place for a comparative assessment of these and the many other options available today for leadership development in the church. Congregations usually wish to make those assessments for themselves. What can be attempted here is a summary of the distinctive characteristics of covenant discipleship groups, and how they complement many other features of congregational ministry and mission.

First of all, covenant discipleship groups are not where discipleship happens, but where people make *sure* that it happens. They are not Bible study groups, prayer groups, share groups, outreach groups, or action groups. All of these can be vital components of congregational life, using the wide array of available materials. Covenant discipleship groups, on the other hand, ensure that there are persons in a congregation who follow the teachings of Jesus in a balanced way, according to the General Rule of Discipleship. The weekly accountability gives their members a regular "compass heading."

Another distinctive characteristic of covenant discipleship groups is that they require an openended commitment. As we have noted, many people balk at this in a climate of small group programs with limited commitments of a month, two months, six months, or even a year. By contrast, covenant discipleship groups stipulate the same commitment Jesus asked of his first disciples: no limits at all.

LEADERSHIP ORIENTED

People who are ready to make this sort of commitment will join a covenant discipleship group. People who are not yet ready will opt for some other way of fulfilling their obligations to Jesus Christ. From the preceding chapters, it should be clear that this is totally in keeping with the working of God's grace, and in no way implies a classification of people's relationship to Jesus Christ. But it does make clear that people respond to God's grace in different ways, and that we should not attempt to homogenize their responses. Covenant discipleship is the response of potential leaders in discipleship who are ready to hold themselves mutually accountable for their walk with Christ. Once they take this step, there is no turning back—and no planned obsolescence.

INTEGRAL AND COMPLEMENTARY

This is why covenant discipleship complements all of the dimensions of congregational life and work. It is also why many other programs and activities need to be in place alongside covenant discipleship. Mutual accountability for its own sake is quite pointless, and covenant discipleship groups by themselves would be spartan and self-defeating. The accountability of the groups is for a purpose: the forming of faithful disciples, and holding them on course as they live out their discipleship in the world. To change metaphors, if covenant discipleship is the "muscle" of the body, there must be a body for the muscle to empower.

THE PRESENCE AND POWER OF
COVENANT DISCIPLESHIP

When covenant discipleship groups are recognized for what they are—a means of grace for the whole body of the church—congregations that initiate and foster them as part of their life and work are infused with more of God's grace. Members of covenant discipleship groups are no more virtuous than their fellow church members; nor are the groups any more a means of grace than the many other gifts which God bestows on a congregation. But they are additional and powerful means of grace. For when there are members of a congregation who open themselves methodically and accountably to God's gracious initiatives, then grace is bound to move more consistently through the body as a whole.

Needless, to say, the signs of this grace are not immediately self-evident; nor is this a dimension of covenant discipleship groups that can be too readily assumed. But it is a deep spiritual truth that congregations become more spiritually attuned to the will of God, and more healthy in all aspects of their discipleship, when their leaders hold themselves accountable for obeying the teachings of Jesus Christ. And in turn, such congregations become more effective channels of grace for the communities in which they witness and serve.

Chapter Six

Covenant Discipleship Groups In the Life of the Congregation

NURTURING COVENANT DISCIPLESHIP GROUPS

One of the strengths of covenant discipleship groups is that they require relatively little direct supervision. Their agenda is focused on what members are doing about their Christian living in the world, centered on the General Rule of Discipleship—acts of compassion, justice, worship, and devotion—and this gives their weekly meetings a structure within which they can reliably hold each other accountable and respond to the power of the Holy Spirit.

Even so, covenant discipleship groups do not just happen. They need to be cared for, just like any other small group in the congregation; and if they are ignored, they will gradually cease to function. For one thing, the very format of covenant discipleship groups—a routine and repetitive series of questions and answers—makes them very susceptible to boredom and loss of interest on the part of some or all of the members. Indeed, groups should expect such times of dryness and emptiness, which some have called the doldrums. If nothing is done to help a group through such a time, it may well lose its sense of purpose.

HEIGHTENED EXPECTATIONS

By the same token, the agenda of covenant discipleship raises the expectations and widens the horizons of group members. There is a high level of commitment when they begin their weekly accountability. They are embarked on a journey with Christ which opens them to new possibilities for their discipleship, and accordingly, they need new opportunities for acts of compassion, justice, worship, and devotion. If these opportunities are not provided through the ministry of the congregation, covenant discipleship groups can easily become self-centered and introspective, more concerned with their heightened expectations than with living out

105

their discipleship. This in turn will leave them frustrated with their weekly process of accountability, because their meetings will tend to be a litany of what they know they ought to be doing, but are not doing—the very self-destructive circle the groups are designed to avoid.

For all these reasons, covenant discipleship groups need to be "watched over in love" no less than their individual members. The following ideas have proved effective in a number of different congregations, and can be used or adapted for particular contexts.

CONVENERS

We have already referred to the role of conveners in the administration of covenant discipleship groups (see above, p. 92). They are a very significant liaison, providing a ready access to all of the members, and serving as a link between the groups, the pastoral staff, and the congregation as a whole.

Where there are a number of covenant discipleship groups, it is helpful to hold a regular meeting of the conveners. This provides an arena in which the progress of the various groups can be monitored. Suggestions can be made for providing groups with opportunities to exercise their discipleship in new ways, resources can be shared, and problems can be discussed. It is by no means uncommon, for example, to have a group shaken out of its doldrums by learning what another group has done when faced with the same difficulty.

COORDINATORS

When the groups have become well established, it is a good idea to appoint a layperson as *coordinator* for covenant discipleship in the congregation. This person can work with the pastoral staff in providing administrative support for the groups, and can also preside at meetings of the conveners. When a coordinator is appointed, the position should be incorporated into the administrative structure of the congregation as a means of linking it with the wider ministry and mission of the church.

THE QUARTERLY MEETING

In addition to regular meetings for the conveners, it is helpful to hold meetings from time to time for all group members; and in some congregations, this has become a quarterly event. The meeting can take various forms, but is primarily an opportunity to provide additional resourcing for the groups. Guest speakers can be invited to address a particular area of discipleship in some depth, and direct the members to further opportunities for service. The General Rule of Discipleship can serve as a guide for these addresses, so that acts of compassion, justice, worship, and devotion receive due attention in turn.

THE COVENANT MEAL

Another form for plenary meetings is the *covenant meal*. This can be held in conjunction with a quarterly meeting, or on its own, and has emerged in recent years as a significant means of grace in congregational life. The meal is sacrificial, with very simple food, and is followed by a time of sharing around the table, during which group members tell stories of discipleship, out of their own experience or that of other Christian disciples. The atmosphere is similar to the early Methodist *lovefeast*, as the stories affirm the boundless nature of God's grace. And on those occasions when Christians from other countries are present, particularly Third World countries, the testimonies are all the more powerful and eloquent.

The covenant meal is also a time for the sharing of pain and suffering, most especially the hurts of the world beyond the congregation which might otherwise remain comfortably hidden and obscure. Thus it is appropriate to take up an offering at the end of the meeting, inviting people to contribute what they would otherwise have paid for a full meal, to be used for the work of the church among the poor and the hungry.

Another important function of the covenant meal is that it provides the opportunity to invite prospective group members to experience covenant discipleship in a very direct way. For those who have shown interest, but have not yet made the decision to join a group, meetings such as this are an open and nonthreatening introduction to the nature and purpose of covenant discipleship. They see the interaction of the members; they hear the stories of discipleship coming out of the groups; they experience the presence of the risen Christ as faithful disciples gather around a meal table in his name; and they are blessed by the inviting grace of the Holy Spirit.

RECRUITMENT OF NEW MEMBERS

The covenant meal is not the only means of recruiting new members for covenant discipleship. Indeed, once the groups are functioning in a congregation, there should be regular invitations extended by the group members and by the pastoral staff. This can be done in any number of settings: from the pulpit, in Sunday school classes, at midweek meetings, and in all of the informal contacts of congregational life and work.

There are two conditions for receiving new members into a group. The first is that they understand the nature of the commitment and are willing to accept the covenant the group is using. There are regular opportunities for changing the covenant, but welcoming a new member is not one of them. This is not to deny new members full participation in the group, and certainly not to place them on any kind of "probation," but rather to introduce them to the mutual accountability of covenant discipleship. The opportunity to share in subsequent revisions of the covenant will soon follow.

The second condition is that prospective new members should be asked to attend the group for three meetings before making the decision to join. During these visits, they should be given the option of taking part in the process of accountability or merely observing. At the same time, prospective members should be limited to three visits before being asked to make their decision. The format of the weekly meetings is such that unlimited participation of those who are undecided will quickly prove disruptive, whereas limited visits of this nature can readily be assimilated.

As we have noted, the only time a covenant discipleship group is closed is during the pilot year. Thereafter, new members may join at any time, and should be encouraged to do so. It is fundamental to the role of the groups in a congregation that they not be perceived as a hidden or mysterious activity, but as an open and continual opportunity for making a contribution to the life and work of the church of Jesus Christ. It stands to reason that if those who first joined the groups had reached a point in their walk with Christ where they needed to take another step forward in their commitment, others are going to reach the same point and will be ready to respond to the same invitation when it is regularly extended.

COVENANT SUNDAY

An excellent opportunity for inviting people to join a covenant discipleship is Covenant Sunday, a Methodist tradition which has been neglected in recent years, but which is now being revived in a number of congregations. The tradition goes back to John Wesley and the annual Covenant Service he instituted for the early Methodist societies. The order of worship, most of which was taken from the writings of two Presbyterian ministers, Joseph and Richard Alleine, has been revised several times since Wesley first published it in 1780. But it remains a powerful and eloquent statement of Christian covenant with God, as can readily be inferred from the prayer of commitment on page 86, taken from the original liturgy.

For many years, Methodists made this a Watchnight Service on December 31. They would gather for worship in the closing hour of the old year so that the first act of the new year could be the renewing of their covenant with God. Later traditions observed it on the second Sunday after Epiphany. Whichever tradition is observed, Covenant Sunday provides an opportunity for some very creative worship, especially in a congregation where covenant discipleship groups are established. Existing groups can review their covenants and publicly renew their commitment; individual members can be asked to give a short presentation to the congregation, testifying to their disciplined commitment and what this has meant for themselves and the mission of the church; and the invitation for others to join covenant discipleship groups once again affirms that they are integral to the life and work of the whole congregation.

REGROUPING

Covenant Sunday is also a good time for groups to review their meeting schedules and, if need be, to change the day and time. It may also be that individual members need to change groups for the same reason. Indeed, some congregations intentionally disband all of their groups prior to Covenant Sunday, thereby allowing members to stay together, change groups if they wish, or form totally new groups. This is especially helpful for groups that have become depleted for any reason during the past year, and need to receive new members.

In summary, Covenant Sunday can be an annual acknowledgment of covenant discipleship groups for what they are: a means of grace for the church. Those who join a group are making themselves accountable for their walk with Jesus Christ, so that through their "methodical" discipleship the whole congregation might better serve the world in ministry and mission. This needs to be affirmed as often as possible, and Covenant Sunday provides just such an opportunity.

COVENANT DISCIPLESHIP
BEYOND THE CONGREGATION

As covenant discipleship has spread throughout the United States and to a number of other countries around the world, it has proved to be adaptable for use in contexts other than the local congregation. The natural habitat of the groups remains the congregation, where they serve to develop leaders in discipleship; but this does not limit them to congregations. The practice of mutual accountability can also be exercised in settings where people come together for other purposes, or where weekly meetings would not be feasible.

CLERGY SUPPORT GROUPS

The most common adaptation of covenant discipleship is for clergy support groups. In many parts of the country, and especially where collegiality is difficult to sustain because of distance, such groups have begun to use covenant discipleship as a component of their meetings. It should be noted that covenant discipleship is not suitable as the sole format of a clergy group. On the one hand, a meeting that lasts for only one hour is not a sufficient reason to take up valuable professional time; and on the other hand, clergy who have traveled any distance to a meeting want to do more than give an account for the basics of their discipleship. When it is the only planned agenda, covenant discipleship tends to be subsumed by other forms of sharing and discussion.

When covenant discipleship is made into a component of clergy support groups, however, it can often be the key to everything else that happens. A time of mutual accountability centered on the General Rule of Discipleship can set a tone for the meeting which enhances other discussion and sharing. This is especially the case when it comprises the first part of the meeting. The intentionality of this opening hour almost always directs the group into richer sharing and exchange.

NOT A SUBSTITUTE FOR THE CONGREGATION

This said, care should be taken not to allow clergy support groups to substitute for covenant discipleship groups in the local congregation, where they are ultimately most productive. While members of clergy support groups can benefit from covenant discipleship in this setting, and learn a great deal about its nature and purpose, they should implement groups in their congregations as soon as possible.

Such a move will have two very positive effects. First, it will direct pastors toward their primary support group—the members of their congregations. By nature, clergy are "congregational animals." This is their calling; this is where they find fulfillment; and if congregational support is lacking, clergy groups will not make up for it. Efforts in this regard are rarely helpful, and can even become detrimental to professional development. On the other hand, a covenant discipleship group has often proved an excellent way of addressing pastoral tensions in a congregation.

Second, belonging to a covenant discipleship group in a congregation as well as to a clergy support group frees the clergy group for deeper professional and personal interaction. Dialogue can be more open, and mutual accountability more particular. If clergy support groups engage in this sort of collegial exercise without being accountable for the basics of Christian living, their discussions become abstract and their agenda progressively introspective. But when the members are holding themselves accountable for these basics through covenant discipleship groups in their congregations, their support groups can then move into areas of discipleship that are uniquely the concern of clergy. Their covenants of discipleship can then focus on the pastoring of their congregations in ministries of compassion, justice, worship, and devotion. Their mutual accountability can open up aspects of their work which need to be shared with trusted colleagues. And they have the sure knowledge that because of the weekly accountability being exercised in their congregational groups, they are not avoiding the basics of their discipleship, but building on them.

SUGGESTIONS FOR CLERGY SUPPORT GROUPS

A clergy support group that incorporates covenant discipleship as part of its meeting might draw from the following suggestions, each of which is designed as a one-hour segment for a monthly meeting. The group can draw on as many of these as it wishes, or for which it has time:

- A covenant discipleship meeting, using a covenant written and agreed by the group. The clauses may be more particular than those of a typical covenant discipleship group, though they should cover all of the dimensions of the General Rule of Discipleship. The role of leader for this hour should rotate, as in other covenant discipleship groups, and mutual accountability should be exercised just as faithfully.

- A report from members of the group on the progress of covenant discipleship groups in their congregations. This should include personal reflections on how the groups are affecting one's own discipleship and that of the congregation as a whole.

- A discussion of some agreed passage of scripture, or a volume of devotional or prophetic literature.

- A time of intercessory prayer, with a diary kept by the group to note concerns and needs.

- A concluding worship service, preferably the sacrament of Holy Communion.

As and when personal sharing grows out of any of these activities, it should be allowed to develop spontaneously. But there should always be a planned agenda, and leadership responsibilities should be assigned on a rotating basis, not only for the covenant discipleship part of the meeting, but for all segments.

OTHER CONTEXTS

These suggestions for clergy support groups can just as readily be incorporated into other contexts. Persons who meet on committees, task forces, commissions, and boards find that an hour of their time devoted to covenant discipleship can greatly enrich their meetings. In some annual conferences, the cabinet and the conference council staff incorporate covenant discipleship into their meetings, holding themselves accountable for their work on behalf of the church. Where meetings are relatively infrequent, as in the case of a national board or committee, some members have agreed to hold themselves accountable by mail or by telephone between their times together. Whatever the context, however, the following principles remain the same:

- Keep the one-hour covenant discipleship format distinct, either preceding or following the other agenda of the meeting.

- Use a shortened covenant suitable for the context of the meeting, but still shaped by the General Rule of Discipleship: compassion, justice, worship, and devotion.

LEADERS IN DISCIPLESHIP

In spite of all these other possible contexts, the most important contribution of covenant discipleship groups is the extent to which they provide leadership in discipleship for congregations. Individual members are, of course, helped personally by their weekly meetings. But the true purpose and function of the groups is to exemplify methodical, reliable discipleship. By holding themselves accountable for witnessing to Christ and for living out his teachings in the world, they can help to form faithful Christian disciples, and help congregations to be more vital in ministry and mission.

If covenant discipleship groups are to provide this leadership, they must be allowed to assume their proper role in the life and work of congregations. Their insights will often be unexpected, sometimes critical, but almost always a source of spiritual discernment on boards and committees, in Sunday school classes, in youth groups, and in the church's ministries of compassion, justice, worship, and devotion. They will not necessarily occupy traditional positions of leadership, but their influence will be substantial—if, that is, they are acknowledged as leaders in discipleship, and if their groups are carefully formed and nurtured.

ALLOWING LEADERSHIP TO EMERGE

To recognize the leadership of covenant discipleship groups is really a matter of common sense. They are the members of a congregation who are *practicing* the discernment of God's will, who are methodically *practicing* obedience. Their accountability week by week gives them a heightened sense of Christ's vision of *shalom*, and a deeper awareness of the promptings of the Holy Spirit which draw us and nudge us toward the reign of God. They need to be heard and heeded as their leadership develops.

Much of this leadership will be implicit in the various ways that covenant discipleship groups participate in the life and work of the congregation. Certain group members, however, are going to develop leadership qualities that are more explicit. Their spiritual discernment will be more sensitive, their knowledge of human beings more astute, their organizational abilities more evident, and their pastoral concern more focused. They will do more than practicing mutual accountability in the tradition of the early Methodist class meeting. They will also be potential pastoral leaders who, working with the staff of the church, can transform a congregation from a flock that constantly demands feeding to a company of disciples who will assist with the *real* work of Jesus Christ: feeding the little ones of the world.

Congregations that recognize such persons for who they are will also want to commission them for what they can do. And this means recovering another important Methodist tradition: the office of class leader.

Part Three

Class Leaders in the Congregation

*Class leaders are laypersons entrusted with the
formation of a congregation in the basics of
Christian discipleship. They do this by helping a
class of fifteen to twenty members shape their lives
according to the General Rule of Discipleship and in
keeping with each one's gifts and graces.*

Chapter Seven

The Need for Class Leaders

THE NATURE AND PURPOSE OF THE CHURCH

To understand the need for leaders in discipleship in our congregations today, we must first be reminded of the nature and purpose of the church. As we explored this theme in Part 1, we found that the church is the sign community of the coming reign of God. It points to the "kingdom of heaven" announced and inaugurated by Jesus of Nazareth: a time of universal love, justice, and peace; a time of *shalom*. As the sign community of this new order, the church is where people are drawn to meet with Jesus Christ and to be reconciled to the family of God; where people are privileged to have a foretaste of God's *shalom;* and where people can learn how to live out the teachings of Jesus in the world.

As they accept and follow these teachings, people are brought into a deepening relationship with God, whose Spirit impels them into the world with a growing commitment to witness to Jesus Christ, and to serve him among the poor and the needy. For the teachings of Jesus make clear that the Holy Spirit will not rest until the fullness of God's salvation extends throughout planet earth. Our hope is in the risen Christ, present in the grace and power of the Holy Spirit. Our challenge is the crucified Christ, present in the sufferings of the little ones who are still being sinned against.

THE UNFINISHED WORK OF JESUS CHRIST

This continuing business of God's salvation is the key to the identity of the church. Christians have the hope of eternal life, and a rich foretaste of it in their community of faith. But they must never forget that the world in which they live is still deeply marred by sin, evil, and suffering. God's salvation will not come to fulfillment without a struggle against the old order of the world, whose powers resist the coming reign of God with demonic force. The unfinished work of Jesus Christ, and also of the church, is to engage in this struggle: a struggle not only against human sin and

117

evil, but also against "the rulers, against the authorities, against the cosmic powers of this present darkness, against the spiritual forces of evil in the heavenly places" (Eph. 6:12).

If the church is to join with Christ in this struggle, it must put on "the whole armor of God" in order to withstand Christ's enemies (Eph. 6:10-17). If followers of Jesus Christ are to be faithful as God's light to the world, as the salt of God's covenant with the world, as God's leaven permeating the world, and as God's seed planted deep in the world, they must enter into the worldly conflict of God's salvation. For they are engaged, not in the maturing of the human race, but in its redemption. They are involved, not in the enrichment of human existence, but in a fight against death. They are not in neutral territory.

PLACES OF DISCIPLINED TRAINING

This engagement against the forces of darkness means that congregations must be places of discipleship, places of disciplined training for serving Jesus Christ in the world. As we saw in Chapter 3, the only way this can be accomplished is for a congregation to be centered on Christ, so that anyone who joins such a company of faith, or merely comes within the sphere of its ministry and mission, will know without any doubt at all what is its business: the business of God's redemption; the business of proclaiming and living out *shalom*. Such a Christ-centeredness does not happen as a matter of course, even when a congregation has many committed Christians in its ranks. Unless specific steps are taken to ensure that Christ is indeed at the center of its life and work, a congregation can quickly become self-preoccupied, serving the needs of its members rather than equipping them to serve Jesus Christ in the world.

In Chapter 2 we saw how this results in the proliferation of church safe houses, where a boundary is drawn between those who belong to a congregation and those who do not, implying that the church dispenses God's grace, as it were, through divine franchise. Quite apart from the self-importance of such a stance, to say nothing of its callous indifference to the rest of the world, the perspective of a church safe house grossly underestimates the resources and the ingenuity of the present world order. This is not the place to discuss the peculiarities of demonic powers. Suffice it to say that congregations which take for granted the freedom of Christian disciples to proceed on their spiritual pilgrimage unmolested have not only lowered their guard and discarded their armor. They have also lost their identity.

INTENTIONAL LEADERSHIP

All of this brings us to the question of leadership. For if congregations are to be faithful in their ministry and mission, they must not only be clear about their identity: They must also have intentional leaders. It is not enough to have competent or even outstanding ministries of worship, preaching, pastoral care, education, healing, spirituality, social outreach, and evangelism. The question is whether these ministries empower people to live out their discipleship in the world. And for this to happen, the leaders of the church must have vision and purpose, and know the reality of their task.

THE PRIMARY TASK OF THE CHURCH

Two writers who have done much to clarify these leadership issues are James D. Anderson and Ezra Earl Jones. In their influential volume, *The Management of Ministry,* they make clear that the purpose of the church is different from that of other community groups or organizations:

> The political party, historical society, and civic club, for example, are formed to do or accomplish something—elect their candidates, preserve the community's heritage, or urge citizen participation in government. The church, however, is people (many of the same people who are members of the other groups) in whose lives God has acted and continues to act. As the church they have no product to sell or cause to support. God is the actor; they have only to be [God's] people.[25]

When God is not acknowledged as the lead actor in the drama of our salvation, congregations tend to vacillate between competing models and identities, leaving their members confused about how they should live in the world as Christian disciples. In the midst of this confusion, programs do little more than foster organizational maintenance, which is precisely what the church should *not* be about:

> The church fails when it exists only to build itself as an institution. Fellowship is not an end in itself but rather a vehicle that people might see the world as it is and live in that world with justice and love.[26]

By contrast, when God is acknowledged as the lead actor in the drama, the primary task of the church emerges with cogency and clarity: to accept people where they are and to relate them to God so that they may truly be God's people in the world. Instead of seeking appropriate forms of ministry for its own sake, the church shapes all of its ministry and mission around its primary task.

MODES OF LEADERSHIP

In a subsequent volume, *Ministry of the Laity,* Anderson and Jones address the implications of this primary task for congregational leaders. Noting the distinction made by James McGregor Burns between transactional leadership and transformational leadership, they argue that both modes are necessary:

> Transactional leaders ask if they are being fair and responsive to their constituents. Transformational leaders ask if they are lifting people above self-interest toward such goals as justice and equality. . . . [They] are often charged with being elitist or rigid—even authoritarian. Some may be, even as transactional leaders may be. The charge against the former, however, often grows out of an inability to differentiate process from vision. Visions do not grow out of least common denominators or easy consensus about what people want changed. . . . Transformational leaders push people toward their central yearnings and then help them reach far enough to position those yearnings as ends to be pursued.[27]

THE NEED FOR
TRANSFORMATIONAL LEADERSHIP

Anyone involved with church leadership today in North America can readily identify with this analysis. There is a preponderance of transactional leadership to the neglect of that which transforms, and thence to the detriment of the church's primary task. Transactional leaders, clergy and lay, are chiefly concerned with the welfare of their constituents. They usually adapt to given situations, with the agreed purpose of maintaining the institutional church. This is not to suggest that institutional maintenance is unimportant. But when it dominates the agenda of the church to the neglect of God's mission in the world, then clearly there is an imbalance in leadership. Put differently, a preponderance of institutional maintenance means that the church has a serious leadership vacuum in discipleship. Faithfulness in this critical area, or lack of it, will always reveal the extent to which the church is or is not centered on Christ.

In these two important concepts—the primary task of the church and transformational leadership in the church—Anderson and Jones point us to the pressing need of North American congregations today. If we are to join with Christ in the unfinished work of God's salvation in the world, we need leaders who will accept responsibility for the discipleship of the church, for the centering of its life and work on the person and the teachings of Jesus of Nazareth. As we have already noted, this centering will not happen as a matter of course. It must be intentionally implemented through the General Rule of Discipleship. Not only, therefore, do we need leaders who will affirm the General Rule. We also need to acknowledge their role in the congregation, and to give them the authority to exercise it.

A CONTEXT FOR
TRANSFORMATIONAL LEADERSHIP

In Part 2, we saw how the Methodist tradition provides us with a context for this leadership—a simple and effective means of mutual accountability for Christian discipleship. Covenant discipleship groups, patterned after the early Methodist class meeting, draw together those members of a congregation who are ready to make a disciplined Christian commitment. Meeting for just one hour a week, they apply themselves to a friendly but firm routine of checking their discipleship with one another. Their covenant is mutually agreed and is written in light of the General Rule of Discipleship, so that they endeavor not only to witness to Christ, but also to walk with him in a balanced obedience of compassion, justice, worship, and devotion.

In this way, covenant discipleship groups create a context for transformational leadership. By holding themselves mutually accountable for their obedience to Jesus Christ, they make clear who is at the center of a congregation's life and work. By their involvement in the various ministries of the congregation, they infuse the membership as a whole with the implications of being a Christ-centered congregation. Their presence on committees, their activity in task forces, and their innumerable conversations and testimonies with other members, all contribute to the identity of the congregation as God's light, salt, leaven, and seed in the world.

IMPLICIT LEADERSHIP

Important though all of this is, it still stops short of what is needed to form congregations into faithful disciples. In and of themselves, covenant discipleship groups cannot provide transformational leadership for the contemporary church. This is because the influence they have in a congregation is implicit rather than explicit. They are not always recognized for who they are and what they are doing. They are a vocational activity within the congregation, so that even when they are carefully introduced and nurtured, they remain a minority. By no means are all members of a congregation ready to make themselves accountable for the discipleship this way. Thus, while the remainder of the congregation will be affected by the witness of these groups, the impact will be indirect. Other members may choose to disregard them.

LEADERSHIP AVOIDED

Indeed, this has proved to be the case in a number of congregations where covenant discipleship groups have begun to present the challenge of costly discipleship. Instead of dealing with the issues being raised, the leaders of the church—and especially the pastor—have adopted a transactional stance, then relegated the groups to just another option in a range of congregational activities.

In this way, confrontation is avoided, but at a price. Instead of developing transformational leaders, leaders in discipleship who will identify Christ as the center of the congregation, covenant discipleship groups are absorbed into the blandness of transactional church programming. They have a continuing influence, but not to the extent they can and should have. In other words, to provide the context for transformational leadership is not enough. A further step is needed: The leadership must be *recognized*.

EXPLICIT LEADERSHIP

If leaders in discipleship are indeed the key to vital congregations, their leadership must be explicit, not implicit. Such intentionality is not likely to sit well in church safe houses, where people are used to the benefits of Christian discipleship rather than the obligations. In congregations such as these, an agreement has usually been transacted with the pastoral staff to provide ministries that affirm God's love—an affirmation, let it quickly be stated, that is altogether in keeping with the gospel of Jesus Christ. The problem is that Christian assurance is only one part of the gospel, and only one mode of congregational leadership. The assurance of God's love must be matched with the call to God's service—a working out of our salvation in Christ Jesus. The leadership that maintains the community of faith as a place of love and belonging must be matched with a leadership that calls this same community of faith to active service of God in the world. Alongside the power of God's love, there must be the ground rules of God's justice, as Jesus himself made clear when he announced his ministry at Nazareth (Luke 4:18-19).

THE OFFICE OF CLASS LEADER

It so happens that the Methodist tradition provides not only the context for such leadership—the class meeting—but also the means by which to exercise it—the office of class leader. The story of how this distinctively Methodist leadership role flourished and was then allowed to decline is told in more detail in the companion volume, *Class Leaders* (order no. DR092B). For the purposes of revitalizing the office today, however, three aspects of its development in the early Methodist societies are particularly important to understand.

First, the position of class leader emerged as a pastoral benefit rather than as an organizational expedient. According to Wesley's own account, the idea came out of a meeting of the Bristol society in February 1742, when society members were discussing how to clear a building debt. The solution they adopted was to divide the membership into subgroupings of twelve, called *classes,* each with a *leader* who would collect the weekly contributions. It was soon found that the regular contact between the leaders and their respective class members also provided pastoral opportunities. In Wesley's own words, the classes were an excellent way of "coming to a sure and thorough knowledge of each person." The leaders were those members of the societies who could "not only receive the contributions, but also watch over the souls of their brethren."[28]

Second, the role of the class leader was disciplinary as much as it was pastoral. Discipleship for the early Methodists was more than doctrinal belief or religious experience. As the name "Methodist" implies, and as Wesley's *General Rules* of 1743 make clear, their priority was obedience to Christ. Class leaders were the ones who saw that this priority was upheld.[29]

This combination of pastoral and disciplinary oversight meant that class leaders had a genuine authority in early Methodism. Not only were they appointed by Wesley or one of his assistant preachers, thereby holding office under an ordained priest of the Church of England. They also came from the ranks of the society members, and were therefore accepted as leaders by their peers.

STEWARDS AND CLASS LEADERS

Third, and perhaps most relevant for the church of today, the role of the class leader was distinct from that of the administrative leadership of the early Methodist societies. This is not to say that class leaders had nothing to do with administration. But the running of the societies rested primarily with the office of *steward*—a word borrowed from the old religious societies of the Church of England.

Stewards were first appointed when, as Wesley put it, he felt "the weight of a far different care, namely, care of temporal things."[30] So he "chose out first one, then four, and after a time seven, as prudent men as I knew, and desired them to take the charge of these things upon themselves, that I might have no encumbrance of this kind."[31] Wesley went on to describe the duties of the stewards:

> To manage the temporal things of the Society;
> To receive the subscriptions and contributions;
> To expend what is needful from time to time;
> To send relief to the poor;
> To keep an exact account of all receipts and expenses;
> To inform the Minister if any of the rules of the society are not punctually observed;
> To tell the Assistants in love if they think anything amiss, either in their doctrine or life.[32]

As we might expect of Wesley, the stewards were further provided with a set of rules:

> (1) Be frugal. Save everything that can be saved honestly.
> (2) Spend no more than you receive. Contract no debts.
> (3) Have no long accounts. Pay everything within the week.
> (4) Give none that asks relief either an ill word or an ill look. Do not hurt them, if you cannot help.
> (5) Expect no thanks from man.[33]

Along with class leaders, stewards met weekly with the preacher of the society—a meeting that was an important link in the structure of the Methodist movement. Since Wesley and his preachers were itinerant, spending little time in one place, local leadership had to be delegated. And the significance of having both class leaders and stewards at this weekly meeting is that Wesley recognized a distinction between administrative and pastoral lay leadership. Both roles had to be delegated; and they were not the same.

A STRIKING PARALLEL

The typology of Anderson and Jones (p. 120) cannot be directly applied to Wesley's societies in retrospect. Too much history intervenes. But the parallel is striking nonetheless: Class leaders and stewards are excellent illustrations of the complementary modes of transformational and transactional leadership.

The transactional leadership of the church that Wesley entrusted to his stewards is very well delegated today. Boards, committees, task forces, and coordinators—all of these abound and often with marked efficiency. Yet by contrast, the transformational leadership he entrusted to his class leaders is conspicuously lacking in our congregations. In spite of many faithful Sunday school teachers, program coordinators, midweek speakers, and outreach facilitators, all of whom contribute much to the knowledge and motivation of church members, Christian discipleship is regarded as a very personal matter, to be determined by each person individually. The result is that, by and large, people are left to work out for themselves how to live as Christ's disciples in the world. They are presented with a multiplicity of programmatic offerings; and if these prove insufficient, the only place to turn for guidance is the pastor or the pastoral staff.

A CRISIS IN TRANSFORMATIONAL LEADERSHIP

Unfortunately, very few pastors or church staff members provide this sort of guidance today. Much is done to structure pastoral ministries, and to provide pastoral counseling at a personal level. But in the basics of Christian living in the world, there is minimal leadership. Not many pastors today know how to form Christian disciples, and those who do know are chronically overworked and seriously underestimated by their congregations and their colleagues. Not only does this leave our ministry and mission severely handicapped. It also deprives our congregational life of any discernible center.

If this leadership crisis is not addressed and remedied, the church in North America will be in grave danger of de-traditioning its discipleship. Each generation of the Christian community depends on the preceding generation to hand on the tradition of faith. There are many ways in which this is done: through the ministries of word and sacrament; through teaching and instruction in the classroom; and through the many intergenerational activities of the church. But most important of all, the faith is traditioned through role models in discipleship, who show by their example what it means to live a Christian life in the world; and these role models are now very few and far between.

SQUANDERED EXPERIENCE

More significantly, the role models we do have are seldom recognized for who they are. They are not encouraged or given the opportunity to share their experience. And let us be very clear what kind of "experience" these people have to offer: learning to live as a disciple of Jesus Christ. This does not come readily or easily. As we have observed more than once, the world is not neutral territory. It requires years of practice to acquire the knowledge and skill necessary to hold one's ground for Jesus Christ and to sustain one's obedience to his teachings—knowledge and skill that have been squandered by the church now for several generations. The resulting vacuum in leadership means that the next generation of Christian disciples is not being prepared to practice discipleship. Before long, there may well be no one to show the new disciples how to sustain their walk with Christ in the world.

Perhaps our biggest mistake in this mis-traditioning is to have placed the role of leading in discipleship beyond the reach of ordinary church members. We have spiritualized discipleship to the point where the average Christian is no longer willing to give or accept advice in how to set about it. Thus we have only two ways of learning how to be a Christian disciple: from our own personal encounters with Christ, or from encounters with spiritual experts. Little wonder we do not delegate leadership in such areas of sensitivity. Even if we did, who would accept it?

SIMPLE TEACHINGS AND COMMON SENSE

Once we look at Christian discipleship from a Wesleyan perspective, however, we see something much more manageable. We see common sense at work, both in our faith relationships with Christ and in following his teachings in the world. We see that faith grows out of works no less than works grow out of faith. More important, we see that our faith and our works develop from small beginnings. Even when our faith is weak, there are things we can do while we wait for it to get stronger. Most important of all, we see that the teachings of Jesus are not superhuman at all, but very simple—so simple that a little child can understand them. What could be difficult about giving food to someone who is hungry, or shelter to someone who is homeless, or comfort and hope to someone who is downtrodden?

The difficulty lies not in the teachings, but in doing what the teachings direct us to do. That is where Wesley's class leaders played such a vital role. They made it possible for early Methodist disciples to *practice* Christian living in the world. They encouraged them, affirmed them, supported them, and helped them. They also advised them, corrected them, rebuked them, and when necessary, rescued them. They "watched over them in love."

PUSHING PEOPLE FORWARD

These are the leaders we need today, alongside the many transactional leaders already in place. To repeat the words of Anderson and Jones, transformational leaders "push people toward their central yearnings and then help them reach far enough to position those yearnings as ends to be pursued."[34] Leaders such as these will talk and dream about the coming reign of God, but they will not stop there. They will also walk and act with Jesus Christ in the world, and impel the rest of the church to do likewise. They will lead and form congregations into vital sign communities of faithful disciples, centered on Christ and Christ alone.

This leadership cannot be the sole prerogative of bishops and pastors of the church, any more than they alone can carry the full load of transactional leadership. The time has come to delegate responsibility for the discipleship of congregations no less than that of administration, and to accord these leaders a full measure of trust so that *all* church members might witness to Jesus Christ in the world, and follow his teachings through acts of compassion, justice, worship, and devotion, under the guidance of the Holy Spirit. In addition to trustees, chairpersons, teachers, and lay leaders, Methodism needs its class leaders.

BACK AFTER FIFTY YEARS

All of this makes it highly significant that in 1988, after an absence of fifty years, the office of class leader was reintroduced into *The Book of Discipline of The United Methodist Church*.[35] It must quickly be pointed out that this absence was not true of Methodism as a whole. There are branches of the Methodist family of churches around the world where class leaders have continued to function, and in some instances with vigor. Notable examples of these are the African and Korean traditions of Methodism, as well as the African-American Methodist traditions, where class leaders and class meetings have long been foundational to church polity and practice. Indeed, it was a Korean district superintendent, Dr. Hae Jong Kim, who drafted the legislation on class leaders and class meetings for the 1988 *Book of Discipline*. The significance of these traditions, and the potential they have for Pan-Methodist cooperation in the future, are dealt with in the companion volume, *Class Leaders*.

The reappearance of class leaders in the United Methodist *Book of Discipline* now provides a signal opportunity for recovering a unique leadership role in the mother church of Methodism. The office had ceased to have any significance in the *Book of Discipline* in 1939, when the Methodist Episcopal Churches, North and South, and the Methodist Protestant Church reunited. Yet the same General Conference had made much of the Board of Lay Activities, an organization that the Methodist Episcopal Church, South had been developing for some time. Its stated purpose in the 1939 *Discipline* was "to deepen the spiritual life of the laymen of the Church and to secure among laymen an increasing loyalty and interest with the ultimate end in view of an active working force in each local Church." The officers were to be conference lay leader, district lay leader, charge lay leader, and church lay leader.[36]

In hindsight, the irony is inescapable. When Methodism first became a church, class leaders were already in place, ensuring that spirituality, loyalty, and faithful activity were normative for Methodists. Yet in spite of many warnings from concerned church leaders,[37] the office had been allowed to lapse, with the result that there was now a need for the laity to be revitalized. The early Methodist circuit riders could have told them as much!

"RE-TRADITIONING" THE OFFICE

This glimpse into history tells us that we should not attempt simply to resuscitate the office of class leader. A gap of fifty years, to say nothing of the several generations prior to 1939 in which the office had been neglected, is too long for a disciplinary clock to be turned back. What we must now do is "re-tradition" the office—that is, understand its role in early Methodism, and then recover and adapt it for the church of today. And first, this means recognizing a number of differences between our context and that of eighteenth- and nineteenth-century England and North America.

FROM SECT TO CHURCH

The most important of these contextual factors is that the office of class leader originated in the early Methodist societies. We have already noted that these societies, with their classes and bands, were *ecclesiolae in ecclesia*—"little churches within the big church." But the point needs to be stressed, because Methodism is now *ecclesia*, not *ecclesiolae*. The Methodist societies of Wesley's day have evolved into a major denominational family. In the social typology of Ernst Troeltsch, they have made the transition from sect to church.[38]

This tradition has profound implications for the self-understanding of Methodism, most especially if we are to understand the office of class leader. Throughout the history of Protestantism, *ecclesiolae*, or little churches, have consisted primarily of laypersons who have committed themselves to a more accountable and even rigorous form of Christian discipleship, usually in the form of small groups. Such was the pattern of the early Methodist societies. But when Methodism became a church, first in the United States of America in 1784, and later in Great Britain and throughout the world, it was impossible to sustain this level of commitment. And today, it means that the disciplinary requirements of the early Methodist societies cannot be applied to the large, inclusive, pluralistic denomination which now comprises The United Methodist Church. If proof of this is required, we need only note that Wesley's *General Rules* are included in the present *Book of Discipline* primarily as a doctrinal statement.[39]

FROM LEADER TO SUB-PASTOR

Another contextual factor governing our re-traditioning of class leaders is the change that took place in the office when Methodism became a church. In the early days of the movement, and for some time after the Methodist Episcopal Church was formed in 1784, pastoral charges were organized into circuits. This was to enable the traveling preachers, or circuit riders, to cover as much territory as possible in proclaiming the gospel and establishing new societies; which in turn meant that there had to be the same strong lay leadership, i.e., class leaders and stewards, that Wesley had fostered in England.

The pioneering era of the circuit rider could not last indefinitely, however, not least because of the physical and emotional demands made on these men. It was inevitable that frontier communities would become settled, and that preachers would wish to give more time to their pastoring and to have their own family life. A clear sign of this is that in 1866, the same year the Methodist Episcopal Church, South discontinued the requirement of weekly attendance at class meetings, the *Discipline* extended from two to four the number of years a pastor could serve in a charge.

These developments brought a significant change to the responsibilities of class leaders. In the earliest *Disciplines* of the Methodist Episcopal Church, their authority was much as it had been in Wesley's societies. But it was not long before the demands of transactional leadership—the responsiveness to church members which necessarily came with the growth of a major denomination—began to weaken and displace the transforming discipline they had once exercised. The change in their role is recounted in more detail in the companion volume, *Class Leaders*. But in essence the change was this: Instead of leading in discipleship, class leaders became sub-pastors of congregations.

FRUSTRATED LEADERSHIP

It remains a fertile area of research to plot these changes in the pastoral shape of Methodism, and to speculate on what might have happened had clergy and laity accepted the challenge of forging a shared leadership of the church. Given the great strength of the tradition of class leaders, the acceptance of such a challenge might well have fulfilled John Wesley's vision of a church truly centered on Christ rather than preoccupied with itself. But instead, the leadership that had hitherto been delegated to the laity was gradually assumed by the pastors; and the grassroots authority of class leaders and stewards was slowly but surely replaced by the clergy-dominated structure of pastorates and annual conferences so familiar to us today.

The need to delegate leadership did not of course disappear. But the nature of that delegation increasingly focused on administration: the transactional areas of church maintenance. At the same time, leadership in discipleship gravitated toward the pastor, whose appointment, albeit itinerant, became a much more permanent fixture, and whose authority in the ministries of word and sacrament became reinforced by the connectional structures of the church.

This trend has continued to the present day. Not only has it caused a dearth of leaders in discipleship. It has also thwarted the call of many laypersons who are ready to assume such leadership roles, and who thus experience deep frustration. Examples abound today in a variety of renewal movements, often in the form of small groups that offer opportunities for a more intentional discipleship. Their emphases range from personal spirituality to radical social justice, and everything in between. As *ecclesiolae,* or little churches, they may or may not function *in* the *ecclesia;* and by the same token, the large church may or may not pay them much attention, or even acknowledge them.

In some ways these movements act as safety valves, allowing frustrations to boil over. In other ways they are genuinely helpful to the persons who participate in them, and thereby indirectly enrich congregational life. But all too often they are an expression of thwarted leadership, which tends to foster an alienation toward congregations and pastors who refuse to recognize their yearnings and their potential. In turn, they are frequently regarded by the transactional leaders of the church as divisive elements—a familiar criticism to any serious student of Wesley.

LEADERS IN DISCIPLESHIP

As we recover the tradition of class leaders, we should do all we can to avoid furthering such frustrations. The office must have integrity of leadership, and must not be seen merely as a way of "helping the pastor look after the congregation." That would merely reinforce the transactional leadership imbalance that already disables so many of our congregations. In any event, the programmatic activities of most congregations already provide a great deal of mutual support and fellowship. And while there are many genuine needs in the average congregation, most church members do not require "sub-pastoring." If the truth be told, many church members do not want to be sub-pastored. They don't *like* to be sub-pastored.

What most church members do want and need, on the other hand, is guidance in how to live out their discipleship in the world more effectively—the very dimension of leadership that class leaders can bring back to the church. This does not mean a return to the discipline of the early societies. A large inclusive church must be open and sensitive to a wide range of faith commitment among its members. But by the same token, if a congregation is to be truly a means of grace, centered on Jesus Christ, and guiding those who want to follow his teachings in the world, then it needs leaders who can help all of its members grow in their discipleship—the tradition we have in the office of class leaders.

METHODISM FULL CIRCLE

Needless to say, all of this will require a major adjustment in the pastoring of congregations. Yet these leaders in discipleship are waiting in the wings, and are ready to take the stage, if only the clergy will acknowledge them as colleagues. To do so could result in the transformation of contemporary ministry and mission. Preaching, teaching, counseling, prophesying, and much more, would not only be a means of visioning the gospel, but could also be translated into practical possibilities for discipleship.

For this to happen, clergy must delegate pastoral responsibility to trusted laypersons, just as they already delegate administrative and programmatic responsibility. They must allow transformational leaders to emerge no less than those who are transactional. There is no better way to do this than to recover the office of class leader, and thus bring Methodism full circle.

HESITATION TO SHARE LEADERSHIP

Even so, many pastors will hesitate to share these pastoral responsibilities. They will find it difficult to trust laypersons with such a critical role in the life of the congregation. Nor will such hesitation be new. The role of lay leadership has always been a sensitive issue in the church; indeed, the trustworthiness of class leaders was one of the first objections voiced against Wesley's introduction of the office.[40]

The problem is exacerbated in North America today by the present theological climate of Protestantism—a polemical climate that can be traced back to the fundamentalist controversies in the early years of this century. The issues that caused these deep disagreements in the church, setting pastor against pastor, and clergy against laity, are no longer at the cutting edge of contemporary ministry and mission. But their legacy of divisiveness still causes mischief, particularly when it comes to defining the nature and the practice of Christian discipleship. At best this distracts congregations from their proper task of serving Jesus Christ in the world. At worst it involves members of the Body of Christ in the distasteful business of questioning each other's credentials.

ESSENTIALS AND NONESSENTIALS

This is where John Wesley can help us once again. Theological controversy was one of the burdens he had to bear throughout his ministry; and it must be conceded that more than once he entered into the fray with inappropriate gusto. But time and again we find him insisting that if the *essentials* of the gospel are agreed, and if the basics of Christian discipleship are practiced, most theological disputes prove to be peripheral.

His sermon, "Catholic Spirit," is best known for the words, " 'If thine heart is as my heart', if thou lovest God and all mankind, I ask no more: 'Give me thine hand.' "[41] Yet he makes clear in the sermon that he is not advocating theological indifference. His argument is rather that if Christians are agreed on the essentials of the gospel, and just as important, if they are doing what Jesus commanded them to do, they are much more likely to be open to the manifestations of God's grace in other people.

The same principle holds true for Christian disciples today. When they are agreed on the basics of what Jesus taught, and are following his commandments by feeding the hungry, clothing the naked, visiting the prisons, caring for the sick, taking good news to the poor, and practicing God's justice toward all, there is rarely dispute among faithful Christians. The *real* disputes then emerge for what they are: disputes with the present world order as we engage the forces of evil.

But when we wrangle over the essentials of the faith, and procrastinate over the basics of our discipleship, then it is not long before our congregations lose their identity, and our church leadership jostles for position, all the while engaging in pointless polemics. And in due course, the polemics become a viable excuse for avoiding the more practical—and obvious—aspects of our Christian duties.

WAITING TO BE ASKED

The whole point of shared leadership in discipleship, therefore, is not doctrinal instruction or theological uniformity, but *application to the task in hand:* acts of compassion, justice, worship, and devotion. In equipping their congregations to follow this General Rule of Discipleship, pastors will find that their most natural support group has been there all the time—leaders who have been waiting to be asked to give a hand. In fact, they have been waiting for several generations.

Chapter Eight

Introducing Class Leaders

LEADERSHIP BY EXAMPLE

The watchword for class leaders is *leadership by example*. This is not to say that persons who hold the office must be paradigms of excellence in Christian discipleship. But it is to say that their commitment to Christ and their efforts to follow his teachings in the world should be such that other church members feel able to look to them for guidance and advice.

Clearly there are gifts and graces particularly suited to such a leadership role; and just as clearly there must be training for the job. But aptitude and training will not ultimately determine the appointment of class leaders. For one thing, to possess the gifts and graces for the office does not mean that a person will necessarily accept its responsibilities. Quite apart from constraints of time, not everyone with such talents is ready to put them to use (Matt. 25:14-30). Then there are those who feel they have these gifts and graces, but who may be less than perceptive in their self-assessment. A sense of assurance is an important blessing of the Christian life, but is not necessarily a qualification to lead in discipleship.

Nor yet should it be assumed that good instruction will necessarily result in good class leaders. While learning how to do the job is important, it does not guarantee that a person will be accepted as a leader. Church members are rightly cautious about following those who are long on training but short on experience.

The only sure credential for class leaders is the example of their own discipleship. Persons who share the common pilgrimage of the congregation, yet who are clearly intentional about their obedience to Jesus Christ, are much more likely to gain the confidence and respect of their fellow Christians than those who are merely gifted or trained.

COVENANT DISCIPLESHIP GROUPS, CLASS LEADERS, AND CLASSES

We saw in the previous chapter why congregations that are concerned about Christian formation need class leaders as well as covenant discipleship groups. While the groups provide significant role models in faithful discipleship, they are insufficient in and of themselves to lead a congregation. Their impact is significant, but ultimately indirect, because not everyone is ready for such an intentional commitment. If accountability for Christian living is to be extended to all church members, there needs to be a direct link between covenant discipleship groups and the congregation as a whole.

Class leaders provide that link by extending the General Rule of Discipleship to other church members, at whatever stage of the Christian journey these members happen to be. They do this by helping a "class" of fifteen to twenty persons with the basics of their discipleship. In this way, all persons in the congregation learn at their own pace how to witness to Jesus Christ in the world, and to follow his teachings through acts of compassion, justice, worship, and devotion, under the guidance of the Holy Spirit.

By the same token, however, class leaders themselves require nurturing in discipleship. If they are to lead others, they must be accountable for their own walk with Christ and, just as important for their credibility with the other church members, they must be *seen* to be accountable. In other words, they need a support base within the congregation. This is precisely what covenant discipleship groups provide. Meeting each week in mutual accountability, they create a context in which class leaders can be sustained in their task of leading the congregation in discipleship. Both of these modes of leadership are important for Christian formation—the implicit role of covenant discipleship groups, and the explicit role of class leaders.

SOME NECESSARY DISTINCTIONS

At this stage, it may be helpful to explain how covenant discipleship groups, class leaders, and classes complement each other, and are also distinct. For one thing, we are using words from the Methodist tradition that have not always carried the same meaning across the years. For another thing, there are many kinds of small group ministries in the church today, and many ways in which we use the word *class*. We need to be very clear about all of this before we proceed.

1. *Not everyone who is in a covenant discipleship group is going to be a class leader.*

There are various reasons why becoming a class leader should not be expected of everyone who is in a covenant discipleship group, and certainly not required. Class leaders are persons entrusted with helping to form the discipleship of other church members, a role which demands focused attention and much prayer and concern. There are bound to be members of covenant discipleship groups who are not ready to help other people in this way; there will be others who feel that this is not their calling; and there are going to be those who would like to be class leaders, but who do not have the time to devote to the task.

The invitation to become class leaders should therefore not be pressured. Members of groups who decline the invitation should in no way be made to feel inadequate or irresponsible, any more than members of the congregation who are not in covenant discipleship groups should be made to feel inferior about their own walk with Christ.

2. *Everyone who is a class leader should be in a covenant discipleship group.*

While membership in a covenant discipleship group does not necessarily lead to the office of class leader, the reverse should hold true: All class leaders should be in covenant discipleship groups. If someone who accepts the office is not yet in a group, he or she should be asked to join one as soon as possible.

There are various advantages to this requirement, the first of which is the obvious value of a weekly time of mutual accountability. In this way, class leaders are seen to be exercising a responsible check on their own discipleship. Just as important, they are seen to be doing so with common sense and objectivity. There is nothing secretive about a covenant discipleship group. There is no required initiation, no extraordinary faith experience, no advanced knowledge of the spiritual life, no radical involvement in social issues. Anyone can join who is ready to be accountable for her or his discipleship according to the basic teachings of Jesus of Nazareth— no more, no less.

For class leaders to be seen to belong to such a group removes much of the apprehension about the office. Since covenant discipleship is open to anyone in the congregation, class leaders are not perceived as an exclusive grouping, but rather as colleagues who are doing a job for the church. Their purpose is seen to be that of advancing the teachings of Jesus Christ, and not the acquisition of personal prestige or privilege.

3. *The "classes" led by class leaders are not the same as covenant discipleship groups.*

Not only are the "classes" assigned to class leaders very different from Sunday school classes, they are also different from covenant discipleship groups. They are pastoral subdivisions of the congregation, comprising fifteen to twenty persons who agree to accept the help of a class leader in living out their discipleship. These classes are not required to meet every week. Indeed, they are not required to meet at all. They are called classes simply because they have a class leader—or more accurately, their members have a class leader. For the class leader relates to the members of the class individually, helping each one with the General Rule of Discipleship according to his or her particular needs.

Moreover, belonging to a class (i.e., being assigned to a class leader) does not carry with it the obligation to join a covenant discipleship group. As we have noted, that is an obligation for the class leader—but not for the class members. Of course, joining a covenant discipleship group is an important step for a class member to take, and should be welcomed by the class leader. But it should happen as and when a person is ready, with no pressure brought to bear at all.

4. *There may be some confusion at first until people understand the difference between "classes" and "class meetings."*

As we have already noted, class leaders and class meetings have been retained in a number of Methodist traditions, most notably the African-American and Korean traditions, and there has been a great deal of interest in class meetings because of small group ministries throughout the church. There may well be some initial confusion, therefore, about the definitions being used in this volume for class leaders and classes, further compounded by the fact that covenant discipleship groups are likewise an adaptation of the early Methodist class meeting.

Do not be discouraged by this confusion. Regard it instead as an opportunity for teaching and learning. As we have stressed, the Methodist tradition does not offer quick and easy solutions for Christian discipleship, but rather gives us methods—if, that is, we will do our homework and *adapt* these methods for the church of today.

This is what we have tried to do on all three counts, with covenant discipleship, class leaders, and classes. Covenant discipleship groups are patterned after Wesley's early class meeting, and are designed for leaders in discipleship. Class leaders for today are patterned after the office that developed when Methodism became a church, and when class leaders were responsible for much of the pastoral oversight of congregations. The classes assigned to class leaders today are not convened as class meetings (see below, p. 158) because the average North American congregation already has plenty of small group meetings, not to mention adult Sunday school classes. These adjustments and distinctions will take time to come into focus; but far better that a pastor and a congregation should struggle with them than try to take a shortcut through history.

5. *Covenant discipleship groups provide a common ground for pastors and class leaders to center their leadership on Christ.*

Just as covenant discipleship groups provide a context in which class leaders and other members of the congregation can share in mutual accountability, they also provide a common ground for the pastor to share in that accountability. The pastor should already be a member of a covenant discipleship group—a requirement of forming the groups in a congregation—and when class leaders are introduced, the importance of this stipulation becomes even more apparent.

Quite apart from the collegiality which it fosters week by week (see below, p. 154), there is the deeper theological issue of where the life of a congregation is centered. By focusing each week, not on who the members are, or what is their faith, or how their spiritual life is deepening, but rather on what they have *done* for Jesus of Nazareth in the world, covenant discipleship groups make Christ the center of their meetings. It is Christ who calls them to accountability. It is Christ who forms their discipleship. And if the pastor is meeting week by week with other leaders in such a context of Christ-centeredness, then it is much more likely to be Christ who provides their congregation with direction and purpose.

By contrast, when the leaders of the church, clergy or laity, become more concerned with leading the church than with obeying the Christ for whom the church exists, then congregations quickly become self-preoccupied, and neglect the transforming disciplines of his teachings. Ordained clergy have been particularly prone to this error, as church history painfully demonstrates; but laity have been no less susceptible to churchly self-preoccupation. If pastors, class leaders, and other committed disciples are meeting together in mutual accountability, they are adopting the best possible safeguard against the most corrupting yet most widespread misconduct of the servants of God: usurping center stage from the Christ they claim to follow and to serve.

6. *Before introducing class leaders, a congregation should have covenant discipleship groups in place for at least two years.*

In order to have a context for mutual accountability firmly established in a congregation, covenant discipleship should be introduced at least two years before the office of class leader: the first year for pilot groups, leading up to a covenant discipleship weekend when the groups are opened to the whole congregation; the second year to allow the groups to become an accepted dimension of the ministry and mission of the church, and thus a supportive base for the class leaders.

During these two years, the pastor should make clear that the intent is to move the congregation toward the appointment of class leaders. It is possible that a few of the members will have memories of the office—those who were fortunate to grow up in churches where class leaders did not completely disappear. In the great majority of United Methodist congregations today, however, the concept will have to be completely reintroduced and people re-educated about its importance in the life and work of the church.

Covenant discipleship provides an excellent setting for this re-orientation. As group members become accountable for their discipleship, they begin to see how helpful it would have been to have had such guidance in their formative Christian years—and how important it therefore becomes to extend this opportunity to others. Discussions about class leaders will not be difficult to generate. And if the pastor is keeping in touch with all of the covenant discipleship groups through quarterly meetings and covenant meals (see above, p. 106), the context of accountability they foster can become a climate throughout the congregation in preparation for the appointment of the first class leaders.

WHEN TO BEGIN

While two years of covenant discipleship is the recommended groundwork for introducing class leaders, it is entirely a matter of pastoral judgment when to take the first step. It should already be clear that without the full understanding and support of the pastor, any attempt to implement the office will not only fail, but will probably cause serious tensions in the congregation. If class leaders are to assume their proper role, therefore, the pastor must be ready to accept a shared pastoral leadership, and the congregation must be ready to accept pastoral guidance from fellow church members who are appointed to the office. Only when there is a willingness on the part of pastor and people alike to make these adjustment should the following steps be taken.

PRELIMINARY PRESENTATION

It is advisable to begin with a preliminary presentation to the administrative board or council. A major innovation such as this will need full discussion, and the decision-making bodies of the congregation will need to feel a sense of ownership. Indeed, there may be the need for several presentations in order to gain support, and all the necessary time should be taken for these.

If the covenant discipleship groups have prepared the ground well, the concept of accountability will not be new to the congregation, and these discussions will be primarily for clarification and assimilation of the idea. If there is serious opposition, however, it will probably be as well to postpone the introduction for a period. During the interim, there can be a more intentional effort to let the rest of the congregation know about the nature and purpose of class leaders, and the necessity of covenant discipleship groups as a foundation of accountability. It may be that the groups need to recruit from a wider range of the membership; and they may also need to be more proactive with the guidelines of the General Rule of Discipleship.

OFFICIAL PROPOSAL

If the preliminary report is well received, the next step is to make an official proposal to the congregation. This should be done at the annual charge conference, or at one that is specially convened, rather than at a meeting of the administrative board or council. Apart from the fact that the *Book of Discipline* stipulates the appointment of class leaders by charge conference, this brings the issue before the whole congregation and gives an opportunity for the widest possible approval. For the same reason, the congregation may wish to make this a church conference rather than a charge conference in order to extend the vote to all church members who wish to attend.[42]

FURTHER PREPARATIONS

Once a charge or church conference has approved the proposal, there are still further preparations. First, the pastoral staff should attend one of the ten-day introductory seminars designed to provide pastors with theological principles and practical guidelines for introducing class leaders. These are sponsored each spring by the General Board of Discipleship in conjunction with a United Methodist seminary or school of theology, and are scheduled to provide a time for reading and reflection as well as lectures and discussion.

Following this seminar, pastors should give serious and prayerful consideration to identifying prospective class leaders. Even though appointment to the office is the prerogative of charge conference, the invitation to consider it will almost always come from the pastor. This is not to say that suggestions cannot and will not be made from other quarters. Still less is it to imply that election at the charge conference will be a formality. But the process of recruitment should include thorough consultation, as with any office of this importance in the life and work of a congregation, and the pastor is well placed to do this.

Since the introductory seminar is held in late spring, invitations can be extended to prospective class leaders at a leisurely pace during the summer months, giving time for people to consider their responses carefully. Those who accept should then be presented to the fall charge conference for election, and officially commissioned on Covenant Sunday in the new year (see below, p. 151).

RECRUITING CLASS LEADERS

The first people to be approached should be those members of covenant discipleship groups who show potential for the office. They will be aware of the decision to introduce class leaders, and will have a good understanding of the nature and purpose of what is involved. Moreover, as the congregation has proceeded in this direction, it is likely that a number of them will have sensed God's call to accept these additional responsibilities. The fact that they have been meeting in their groups for two years or more makes this a natural development in their own discipleship, and for such persons the invitation of the pastor will be very much a mutual recognition of their call. There is more about this in the companion volume, *Class Leaders*.

As we have noted, however, by no means everyone in a covenant discipleship group will wish to be a class leader, or will have time for the responsibilities. Accordingly the pastor should not limit the invitation to covenant discipleship members. There will be others in the congregation well suited for this work, and some of them will be readily identifiable: members who have shown commitment to the teaching ministries of the church; who have taken part in intensive Bible studies and other forms of renewal; who have taken a lead in community outreach; who have sought a more disciplined spiritual life; who have advocated and worked for peace and justice in the world.

Indeed, anyone who has shown intentionality about her or his discipleship is a prospective class leader. Those who are serious about serving Jesus Christ in the world, never mind how much they themselves still have to learn, are the ones who can best be trusted to lead others in their walk with Christ. Even if someone has tended to focus on one aspect of discipleship to the neglect of other duties and responsibilities of the Christian life, that is no reason to discount this person's potential as a class leader. Participation in a covenant discipleship group will quickly balance one's leadership with all the dimensions of the General Rule.

POTENTIAL AMONG YOUNG PEOPLE

While giving consideration to prospective class leaders among the adult members of the congregation, it should not be forgotten that young people will also show potential for the office. Those responsible for Branch Groups (covenant discipleship groups for youth) and for covenant discipleship groups on college campuses should let these young people know that becoming a class leader is a real possibility for their future discipleship, and be ready to nurture this potential leadership among their group members. (See the companion volumes, *Branch Groups* and *Covenants on Campus*.)

POTENTIAL FOR FULL-TIME MINISTRY

One further word needs to be said about this process of recruitment. It is not at all unlikely that the call to become a class leader will be the first step toward a call to full-time ministry. In Wesley's day many class leaders went on to become itinerant preachers, and as the office once again becomes part of our congregational life, we should expect the same progression. In approaching women and men about the office, and in letting young people know about its possibilities, pastors should be ready to discern this further call, and nurture it with great care—and joy.

REALISTIC EXPECTATIONS

Having established that example rather than expertise is the most important credential for class leaders, we must still ask whether there are personal qualities expected of those who hold the office. The answer, of course, is yes. From the very beginning of the office, there have been expectations of class leaders. The Minutes of the earliest Methodist Conferences, and the subsequent Methodist *Disciplines,* have all stressed the importance of commitment to Jesus Christ, spiritual gifts, sound character, faithfulness in meeting obligations, and loyalty to the church.

Yet a word of caution is in order. The reintroduction of an office that has long been neglected should not be viewed with unrealistic expectations. It will probably take at least a generation to recover the accountable discipleship that Methodism took more than a century to lose; and it will take a great deal of trial and error to reestablish a tradition of leadership in which standards and ideals can be reliably sustained.

This means that the new generation of class leaders in The United Methodist Church will be tasked, not only with the duties of their office, but also with reestablishing it across the church. They will have to be both practitioners and advocates. They will not be alone in this task, for class leaders from other Methodist traditions will be there to help and advise. But we must not expect too much of these new leaders, nor they of themselves and of those entrusted to their leadership.

With these realistic expectations, we can describe some of the qualities expected of class leaders. The list is not exhaustive, and should certainly not be regarded as a profile. It is rather a set of indicators, to be used with the clear understanding that the Holy Spirit is already at work to prepare them as leaders of the church. These qualities merely help to provide a mutual and spiritual recognition of God's call.

QUALITIES EXPECTED OF CLASS LEADERS

1. *Class leaders should be authentic Christian disciples.*

The word *authentic* is used here in the sense of faithful Christian living. It means knowing what it is to repent and to be reconciled to God through Jesus Christ. It means knowing what it is to receive the inward assurance of the Holy Spirit. It means practicing the General Rule of Discipleship: the spiritual disciplines of worship, sacrament, prayer, Bible study, and fasting; the practical ministries of compassion and justice toward the hungry, the homeless, the sick, and the imprisoned.

But most of all, an authentic Christian disciple is one who knows what it is to strive for obedience to Jesus Christ in the midst of worldly temptations and in spite of countless failures. This knowledge cannot be learned secondhand. It can only be gained by following Jesus Christ, doing the best one can with the grace one is given, and knowing more and more with the passing years that Christ is all in all.

Persons who have this knowledge have the ring of authenticity in their witness to Jesus Christ and the mark of authenticity in their walk with Jesus Christ. They do not merely know *about* Jesus Christ. They *know* Jesus Christ.

2. *Class leaders should be accepting of others.*

Men and women who walk with Jesus Christ and witness to his saving power are the first to acknowledge that God is no less present in the lives of other people. They do not regard their own experience of Christ as the criterion by which everyone else's faith should be measured. They remember their own resistance to God's grace, and how long it took them to surrender to the Holy Spirit's pleading and yearning. They also remember how ungraciously they accepted their reunion with God's family, and how often they have been mistaken in their understanding of God's will.

All of this gives them an openness to the working of the Holy Spirit in the lives of others. Not only do they see an infinite variety of responses to God's grace on the part of Christians; they also see God at work in the lives of those who are not yet Christian. Their own spiritual pilgrimage renders them unwilling and unable to pass judgment on anyone else's response to God's grace—whatever that response might be. This in turn enables them to be a guide and mentor to everyone.

3. *Class leaders should be courteous, yet candid.*

The purpose of the office of class leader is not to shepherd church members, nor yet to provide them with pastoral care. These are important ministries of the church for which there are leaders already in place and some excellent resources available.[43] Class leaders are more concerned with grounding the discipleship of other church members—showing them the ropes, giving them suggestions for the basics of Christian living in the world, and making sure that their discipleship is balanced according to the General Rule of compassion, justice, worship, and devotion.

This means that the relationship between class leaders and church members will focus on what people are doing about their discipleship rather than counseling with them about their personal lives. There will of course be times when the relationship will be deeply spiritual, especially when members of the class are at critical points in their Christian pilgrimage. But most of the advice leaders give to their class members will consist of common sense and practical guidelines. Thus it is far more important for class leaders to practice courtesy and candor than to acquire the more technical skills of pastoral counseling. Class members with these needs can always be referred to professional care.

4. *Class leaders should be blameless in their lives.*

This may seem an obvious statement to make, but it is important nonetheless: Class leaders should be beyond reproach in their personal and social lives. This is not to say they should be subject to unnecessary scrutiny, and certainly not to suggest that they should have to meet unreasonably exacting standards of behavior. But it is to say that there should be nothing in their lifestyle which could be a stumbling block to others.

This is one of the disciplinary questions asked of clergy each year at annual conference, and to the extent that class leaders are to share in the pastoring of the congregations, it is an important question to be asked of them also. It is important, moreover, to ask it of their social as well as their personal lives. The General Rule of Discipleship is concerned with justice and compassion no less than worship and devotion, and if class leaders are to guide other church members in the basics of Christian living in the world, they must be ready to be role models in all four of these areas.

SELF-SELECTION THROUGH COVENANT DISCIPLESHIP

When all is said and done, however, most class leaders will be identified through a process of self-selection. The requirement that they be members of a covenant discipleship group will preclude any who are not willing to assume the office responsibly. It will also preclude any who feel that their particular faith experience qualifies them for leadership, but who are not willing to hold that experience accountable to the General Rule of Discipleship.

This is why it is vitally important that membership in a covenant discipleship group be clearly stipulated as a condition of the office. If the prospective class leader is already in a group, the importance of continuing in weekly attendance must be stressed, even if he or she is the only member of the group to become a class leader. If the person is not yet in a group, then it must be made clear that appointment to the office is conditional on joining one. The reasons for the weekly accountability, and the importance of covenant discipleship for the congregation, should be fully explained. This allows prospective class leaders to see that joining a group is not an arbitrary condition, but is in fact the surest way of developing their leadership. These matters are examined in detail in the companion volume, *Covenant Discipleship.*

REASSURANCE THROUGH
COVENANT DISCIPLESHIP

Having class leaders belong to a covenant discipleship group can also be a means of reassuring persons who are considering the office, but who feel overwhelmed by the responsibilities. They wonder whether they are sufficiently faithful in their own walk with Christ to be able to guide other people with their discipleship, and are therefore reluctant to assume a leadership role.

This reluctance is a healthy sign. But it should not be allowed to inhibit prospective class leaders, and covenant discipleship provides an excellent way of reassuring any who are hesitant on this score. Meeting weekly with other accountable disciples quickly shows them that God's grace ultimately prevails, not only in other people's lives, but in their own as well. In the matter-of-fact format of covenant discipleship, prospective class leaders learn that the Christian life consists of doing the best we can with the grace we are given. And since all credit belongs to Christ, there is no room for false pride—or false modesty.

PILOTING CLASS LEADERS

Even when the pastor has extended invitations to all prospective class leaders, it is likely that at first only a few persons will be ready to accept the office. And since the recommended number of members assigned to a class leader is fifteen to twenty (see below, p. 161), this means that in all probability only a small percentage of the congregation will initially be involved in classes. In other words, the introduction of class leaders will almost certainly be in the nature of a pilot project.

Far from being a handicap, this is the best way to proceed. It means that the congregation can become acquainted with the office gradually, and grow accustomed to its leadership role—just as with pilot covenant discipleship groups. However sensitively class leaders approach their task, and however much they allow for the range of Christian experience in a congregation, church members will probably find it discomforting, if not disconcerting, to be held accountable for the General Rule of Discipleship. For many, it will be an intimidating concept of discipleship. And even for those who remember the "methodical" Methodism of years ago (and who have long extolled its benefits), actually coming to grips with an accountable discipleship may well give rise to second thoughts.

A pilot process can do much to allay these anxieties. By showing how an accountable discipleship is not only the most faithful but ultimately the most rewarding form of Christian living in the world, and by showing people step-by-step how pilot classes can help them to form such a discipleship, pilot class leaders will gain acceptance for the office with much more integrity. They will stimulate interest among church members in a positive and non-threatening way; and they will avoid the imposition of a pastoral superstructure—the last thing we need today in the church. Piloting class leaders means that the office will take root in congregations.

ON-THE-JOB TRAINING

Introducing class leaders through a pilot process is also the best way to provide training for those who will hold the office. While there are weekend workshops sponsored by the General Board of Discipleship, and while there are many additional opportunities for training described in the volume *Class Leaders*, these are all in the nature of continuing education and resourcing. For the fact of the matter is that being a class leader does not require intensive training. Showing people the ropes merely requires the experience of having used the ropes first. The General Rule of Discipleship is not complicated. Acts of compassion, justice, worship, and devotion are very straightforward, and can readily be demonstrated to other people—provided, of course, that one is doing them oneself.

While it is helpful, therefore, for the pastor to spend some time with newly appointed class leaders in establishing a working relationship (see below, p. 156), the most significant training they will receive is "on-the-job"—exercising their office and getting to know the members assigned to them. Their most important qualification is the one they already have: a working knowledge of what it means to be a Christian disciple. And on the great majority of occasions when they need to give guidance to their class members, this is the only expertise on which they will need to draw.

APPOINTMENT OF CLASS LEADERS

The appointment of class leaders takes place at a charge conference of the congregation.[44] If there are special circumstances that make it difficult to do this at the regularly scheduled time, a special charge conference may be called for the purpose.[45] Since a charge conference will already have approved the proposal to move in this direction (see above, p. 142), and since the pastor will have taken great care in extending invitations to the prospective leaders, their appointment will be primarily a vote of confidence on the part of the congregation.

This does not mean, however, that it should be regarded as a formality. The prospective leaders should be asked to make a short statement concerning their call to the office and their understanding of its duties. And while not prescribed by the *Discipline*, it is appropriate to have each of them elected to office by written ballot. As in the certification of candidates for the ordained ministry, the vote should be two-thirds of those in attendance.[46]

AN ANNUAL APPOINTMENT

As with clergy, and as with many other church positions, the appointment of class leaders should be made annually. Everything about the office makes it highly desirable, of course, that persons should hold it for many years—indeed, for a lifetime, or as long as they are able to fulfill the duties. Even so, it is important to have charge conference confirm the appointment each year, and thus give everyone a sense of participation in leadership. By the same token, it reaffirms the accountability of the class leaders to the congregation as a whole.

A further advantage of making appointments an annual process is that it provides an opportunity to review the work of each class leader, and if need be to ask an unsuitable person to step down. The fact that all class leaders are in covenant discipleship groups, and are also reporting to a monthly leaders' meeting, makes it very unlikely that such a step will have to be taken. But the procedural safeguard is there should it be needed.

COMMISSIONING OF CLASS LEADERS

Once appointed, class leaders should be officially commissioned during a Sunday morning worship service. This too should be done annually, and a special liturgy for this occasion is planned for the United Methodist *Book of Worship* (1992). A good time for this is Covenant Sunday, traditionally celebrated early in January, when the service of commissioning can be combined with the annual Covenant Service, also included in the *Book of Worship*.

Covenant Sunday is likewise the time suggested for the annual renewal and recognition of covenant discipleship groups (see the companion volume, *Covenant Discipleship*). The pastoral staff of the church should therefore feel free to form a creative liturgy around all of these themes, building on what is recommended in the *Book of Worship*. The service might include some readings from Methodist literature, especially from the writings of early class leaders, and might also include examples of Methodist discipleship across the years.[47] To have covenant discipleship groups recognized and class leaders commissioned at the same time makes this a truly significant moment in the church year.

After commissioning, the duties of class leaders will not commence immediately. They will first need to study the volume *Class Leaders* under the supervision of the pastor. They will also need to familiarize themselves with the programs and activities of the congregation so that they can provide their class members with every opportunity to develop their discipleship. And they will then need to be assigned their class members. All of this, and more, will be described in the concluding chapter.

Chapter Nine

Class Leaders in the Life and Work of the Congregation

A PASTORAL APPOINTMENT

In order for class leaders to assume their proper role in the life and work of the congregation, it should be understood that from the very beginning the office has been a pastoral appointment. John Wesley assigned the first class leaders himself, and made clear thereafter that they held their position solely at the discretion of himself or one of his preachers.[48] The same was true for American Methodism, where the traveling preacher, or circuit rider, appointed the class leaders in a new society, and where it remained the prerogative of the pastor to appoint or remove them as long as the office was designated in the *Discipline*.[49]

Needless to say, the development of lay leadership to this level of responsibility and pastoral oversight was not without its tensions. But in the early days of Methodism, the tensions were healthy, and were concerned primarily with the living out of Christian discipleship in the world. In matters of dispute, the authority of the preacher lay in the call to full-time ministry and in the knowledge that came from studying the scriptures and tradition of the church; while the authority of the class leader lay in the knowledge of what it meant to live out these teachings in everyday life—the sort of "frontline" witness for Christ that preachers rarely experienced firsthand.

By contrast, in our present climate of predominantly transactional leadership, disputes tend to be centered on issues of institutional power, causing widespread disillusionment among clergy and laity alike, and leading one Third World theologian to characterize those of us in the United States as a clergy-dominated church with a laity-dominated clergy, offering a gospel without demands and making demands without the gospel.[50]

THE CARE OF SOULS

The main reason for this contrast is that the early Methodists were more clearly focused on the proper business of the church: proclaiming the gospel to all who would hear, and nurturing the discipleship of all who would respond. They knew that the time-honored ministry of the care of souls cannot be undertaken thoughtlessly or delegated lightly, so they gave their preachers direct authority over class leaders. If the office is to be revitalized today, the pastor must retain the same direct supervision, even though class leaders are appointed by charge conference.

If this seems to be authoritarian, it should be remembered how carefully and thoroughly we screen candidates for the ordained ministry before their call is confirmed. It should also be remembered that their call is first acknowledged by the same body of the congregation: the charge conference. In other words, the clergy who are to have pastoral authority in the life and work of the church are not given this permission without the recognition and approval of laypersons. Once given that authority, however, they are trusted to exercise it faithfully after proper training and examination.

A great deal of trust is also to be given to class leaders. They too are to nurture and guide other persons in their discipleship. It is right and proper, therefore, that their immediate supervisor should be the one to whom ultimate responsibility for the congregation has been entrusted. If the duties of class leaders were primarily those of administration and program, this supervision would not be nearly so critical. But in areas of discipleship, where the transforming disciplines of the Christian life are focused on obedience to Jesus Christ and the living out of his teachings in the world, leadership is much more a matter of trustworthy guidance—which most assuredly requires pastoral supervision.

ACCOUNTABILITY AND AUTHORITY

In order for leadership such as this to be acknowledged and accepted by the congregation, there must be a clear authority about the discipleship of class leaders themselves. They must be *seen* and *known* to be leaders, in the same way the pastor is seen and known to have been ordained by the church. As we noted in the previous chapter, participation in a covenant discipleship group provides just that visibility and perception: a weekly point of accountability, where discipleship is shaped by a covenant incorporating the dimensions of the General Rule—compassion, justice, worship, and devotion. This, more than anything else, establishes the credibility of class leaders. They are seen to be persons who take their own discipleship seriously, and who will not be asking others to do what they themselves are not attempting.

Even more important, their weekly accountability keeps them very aware that the disciplines of the Christian life are not developed easily, and that any accomplishments in these areas come solely from the grace and power of the Holy Spirit. As a result, their leadership has a quality of understanding and humility which prevents them from having unrealistic expectations of their classes, or from placing undue demands upon them. Because they are accountable for their own discipleship week by week, their authority comes from practical common sense and experience.

PASTORAL COLLEGIALITY

Once this authority is granted by the congregation, the collegiality between a pastor and class leaders has infinite potential. Indeed, for clergy who have labored long under the tensions of transactional power struggles, and for laity who have long been resigned to the frustrations of thwarted transformational leadership, the newfound sense of common vision and purpose can be deeply moving.

When the transforming ministries of light, leaven, salt, and seed are neglected, the repetitive and routine transactions of churchly business quickly impoverish pastoral relationships, leading to general despair and loss of vocation throughout the congregation. But when the transforming disciplines of the Christian life are given full rein through the leadership of clergy and laity alike, grace flows in abundance. When Christ is at the center of the congregation, the gifts of everyone are allowed full expression. When Christ is honored as the head of the body, all parts work together to full mutual advantage.

PASTORAL FREEDOM

A further blessing of this pastoral collegiality is its freedom. When class leaders are recognized and appointed, not only does the congregation feel the impact of their leadership in centering its life and work on Jesus Christ: so does the pastor. Here at last is a group of colleagues with whom to share freely the gifts and graces of his or her call. The years of theological and biblical training take on new meaning when there are those in the congregation with whom to be free about the more particular aspects of pastoral expertise. The weighty issues of ethical and social action become relevant and more practicable when tested and tried against the worldly experience of trusted co-pastors. And the deeper dimensions of the spiritual life become more meaningful when shared openly with those whose chief concern is the discipleship of other church members.

PASTORAL TEAMWORK AND MUTUAL RESPECT

The key to this pastoral freedom lies in a different mode of leadership for pastors. If they are to experience collegiality with class leaders, they must become facilitators of pastoral teams rather than trying to pastor their congregations singlehandedly, or with the help of paid staff. Clearly there are areas in which they must retain full responsibility: the ministries of word and sacrament, for example, or the special needs of pastoral counseling. But just as clearly there are areas of basic Christian discipleship in which the class leader can function as co-pastor, not only competently, but in some instances even more effectively. There are many occasions when people need simply to be shown the ropes, and to have the practical, down-to-earth advice of another layperson.

By the same token, class leaders can help the pastoral staff of the church to learn much more about, and from, their congregations. In point of fact, there are very few church members who are not doing their best to live out their faith in the world—efforts of which the professional staff are often unaware, for no other reason than lack of contact due to lack of time. But with pastoral teams of class leaders in more frequent dialogue with the congregation as a whole, everyday experiences can more readily be shared. This in turn generates mutual respect and trust. Not only do pastor and people come to appreciate one another's insights and expertise, but professional staff come to see the faithfulness of the average church members in a new light. Instead of measuring the worth of their members by what they do for the church, pastors begin to appreciate what their members are doing for Christ in the world.

HEALTHY TENSIONS

If there are tensions between pastors and class leaders in developing this teamwork, they are not likely to arise from determining leadership roles. Once it is clear that the agenda of class leaders is to promote the teachings of Jesus Christ, and that this is the purpose of their relationship with other church members, there is more than enough for everyone to do without worrying about who is in charge. Any tensions that develop will stem rather from the challenges of pastoring a congregation that is more directly in ministry and mission to the world than it has ever been. As in the early days of Methodism, these tensions will be healthy ones.

THE LEADERS' MEETING

After the appointment of class leaders, the first and most important step is to establish a monthly leaders' meeting, which thereafter becomes a priority for the pastoral staff and all class leaders. This meeting is in addition to and quite distinct from the weekly covenant discipleship groups in which the pastor and all class leaders are also involved.

A good time to schedule the leaders' meeting is on a Saturday, beginning with breakfast. Then discussion can flow around the table for as much of the morning as is needed. Each meeting has two objectives: to provide ongoing support and supervision for the class leaders; and to "take the pulse" of the congregation through the reports of the class leaders. While there need be no set agenda, these two objectives should always be given regular attention, and will normally comprise most of what is discussed.

SUPPORT AND SUPERVISION

First, the meeting should provide a supportive setting in which class leaders feel free to share any aspect of their duties with the pastor and with one another. Just as covenant discipleship groups require care and nurture if they are to function as intended, so class leaders need to be supported and affirmed if they are to assume their proper role in the life and work of the church. The most important context for this is the monthly leaders' meeting.

The meeting should also keep class leaders regularly informed about the range of programs and activities available to church members. It will not be enough for them merely to cite the General Rule of Discipleship as a guide for their class members. They will need specific information about how people can *follow* the General Rule: how they can learn to witness to Jesus Christ in the world, and how they can further their discipleship through acts of compassion, justice, worship, and devotion. Discussion of the congregation's programs and activities is also an opportunity for the supervision of class leaders, most of which will prove to be mutual supervision—suggestions for relating to their members more effectively, and the sort of corrections that always come best from an open collegiality.

"TAKING THE PULSE" OF THE CONGREGATION

The second objective of the leaders' meeting is to "take the pulse" of the congregation—to discern from the class leaders where the members on the whole find themselves in ministry and mission. Once the leaders have established a relationship with their classes, this monthly session with the pastoral staff will be a goldmine of information and consciousness raising.

On the one hand, the leaders can report any problems their members might be experiencing. Since their task is not to provide specialized pastoral care, the leaders' meeting can be a means of referring such problems to appropriate professional ministries of the church. On the other hand, this monthly consultation can be a means of identifying other needs among the congregation—quite ordinary needs that are often unmet simply because they are unknown or unrecognized.

DISCERNING CONGREGATIONAL GIFTS AND GRACES

Just as important as learning about members' problems, the leaders' meeting can be a means of discovering a congregation's gifts and graces. Class leaders are going to acquire considerable knowledge in this regard as they help shape the discipleship of their members around the General Rule. In directing their classes toward the ongoing activities of the congregation, and in encouraging them to participate, they will gain a sense of what church members really need in order to develop their walk with Christ.

By sharing these insights at the leaders' meeting, they can help the pastoral staff and the administrative council to plan church programs that address genuine needs and interests, rather than try to discover what will attract people's participation—or worse, using up reserves of goodwill in persuading people to support unnecessary and unwanted activities.

FORMING THE CLASSES

Once the leaders' meeting is functioning, its first major task is to assign a group of church members to each class leader. These pastoral groupings will be known as *classes;* and since this is a common word in the church, it is important to be clear about their nature and purpose.

We noted in Chapter 7 that when class leaders and class meetings were introduced into early Methodism, class leaders were appointed first and were then assigned classes. The sequence is significant, because it indicates that these subdivisions of the early Methodist societies were not so much a small group strategy as a means of implementing leadership. Small group dynamics quickly developed, of course, as the weekly gatherings fostered a spirit of "watching over one another in love." But the classes were formed around the class leaders, and not vice versa, because the purpose of the early class meeting was the fostering of an obedient discipleship. The fellowship that followed was a blessing, not an objective.

CLASSES, NOT CLASS MEETINGS

In assigning classes to class leaders we must keep that purpose clearly in view, because in the average United Methodist congregation of today it will not be necessary to convene the classes as class meetings. It may even be counterproductive to do so, at least for quite some time.

This may seem to part with the tradition we have been at such pains to recover. It may also seem to reject the experience of those branches of Methodism where the tradition of class leaders and class meetings has been kept alive. But in fact it is merely to take note of the transition in North American Methodism from small societies to a large pluralistic church, and also to accept the reality of our present cultural context in the United States.

With regard to our history, we have already noted that when Methodism became a church, the role of the class leader gradually changed from leading in discipleship to pastoring a subdivision of the congregation (above, p. 130). We should also note that the class meeting underwent a similar change. As Methodist congregations grew in size, they found it increasingly difficult to hold to the disciplines of the early societies, and class meetings began to adopt a less demanding agenda. Rather than accountability for the practice of discipleship, the weekly gatherings focused on prayer and testimony, a format that ultimately became stereotyped and then sterile.[51]

This is a timely warning for the church of today, where discipleship is often confused with Christian fellowship, particularly where small groups are concerned. When the objective is accountable discipleship, then the early Methodist class meeting provides an excellent small group model, as in present-day covenant discipleship groups. Such groups are for those who are ready to take their discipleship seriously—persons who, as we noted in Part 1, are always in a minority. Covenant discipleship groups in a congregation rarely consist of more than 15 percent of the active members, or 5 percent to 7 percent of the membership roll.

CLASSES FOR DISCIPLESHIP

On the other hand, when the objective is to help the church membership as a whole to grow in their discipleship, then it is questionable whether the small group format is necessary or even appropriate. Given the wide range of Christian commitment to be found in the average North American congregation, it is unlikely that a common focus on the General Rule of Discipleship could be sustained in a representative small group. There would be too much disparity, too many different concerns, and the result would almost certainly be to opt for a less demanding agenda—precisely what led to the demise of the old class meeting.

Besides this, there are countless other small group activities in congregations today. There are prayer groups, Bible study groups, growth groups, enrichment groups, service groups, action groups, renewal groups, to name but a few. Indeed, therein lies the most dangerous pitfall of trying to reintroduce class meetings along with class leaders: They would be seen as just another small group activity—the last thing most church members want or need right now. Instead of extending the General Rule of Discipleship throughout a congregation, class meetings would be seen as an imposition. Their purpose would be thwarted.

By contrast, if classes can be assigned to class leaders without the necessity of being convened, but merely as pastoral groupings, class leaders will have the freedom and flexibility to help the members with their discipleship, one-on-one, at whatever stage of the

Christian journey a member happens to be. The members will be aware that by accepting assignment to such classes they can be provided with some basic assistance in their daily walk with Christ.

They will also know that their class leaders are persons whose chief qualification for the job is that they are leading the way, not by superior accomplishment, but by holding themselves accountable week by week in a covenant discipleship group. In a word, they will know that their class leaders are trustworthy, and that their guidance can be accepted in full confidence.

DISCIPLESHIP CLASSES AND SUNDAY SCHOOL CLASSES

Another reason for not convening these discipleship classes is that the word *class* is chiefly associated in the United States today with church school or Sunday school—a place where everyone from infants to senior citizens can learn about the Christian faith and at the same time experience a direct and often intimate form of Christian community. Albeit not always and everywhere in good health, the adult Sunday school class is a peculiarly North American phenomenon. Nowhere else in the world does it play such a role in the life and work of the church.

The classes to be assigned to class leaders clearly have a very different purpose. They will be classes for the forming of Christian discipleship, rather than instruction in the faith or assimilation into the congregation. Yet if they were to be convened as class meetings along with the office of class leader, they would be seen as a duplication of much that is already taking place in the Sunday school, and could well cause friction and divided loyalty among faithful church members. If proof of this assessment is required, we need only note that in those branches of Methodism where the traditional class meeting is still functioning, adult Sunday school classes are not nearly so strong—a piece of contextual data that is not always adequately considered when the effectiveness of class meetings is held up as a paradigm for faithful discipleship.

The office of class leader, on the other hand, can readily be revitalized without disturbing the adult classes of the Sunday school, any more than it will disturb the other programmatic and administrative dimensions of the congregation. As we noted in Chapter 7, the classes assigned to class leaders will be complementary to existing church organizations; and far from tampering or interfering with what is already in place, classes and class leaders will be a tremendous source of restrengthening and reinvigoration.

ASSIGNING THE CLASSES

The recommended number of persons to be assigned to each class leader is fifteen to twenty. This is not a hard and fast rule, however, and the size of classes can be determined by the leaders' meeting in consultation with the administrative council or the council on ministries. There are no criteria for class membership, other than the willingness of the person to accept the guidance of the class leader, and that of the leader to accept the person into his or her class.

The assigning of members to the classes should be done carefully, and by no means all at once. We have already noted that the first class leaders will probably be in the nature of a pilot project, and will therefore be too few in number for the whole congregation to be assigned initially. Likewise it may well take time for church members to respond in sufficient numbers to constitute full classes for all the class leaders appointed.

In either event, classes should be formed only as members are willing to accept assignment to the class leaders available. It will take several leaders' meetings to make assignments and reassignments, as prospective members accept or decline, and the process should not be hurried. If it means a modest beginning, that is preferable by far to a superimposed network of leaders and classes, neither of whom are fully aware of what they ought to be doing, and both of whom are thus likely to have a negative experience.

As the leaders' meeting comes to grips with these issues, the following guidelines may prove helpful:

1. *Make each class as representative as possible of the membership as a whole.*
It will be a pastoral temptation to assign the first classes on the basis of "problem members," or "inactives," or "seasoned resisters." This would be a serious mistake. The purpose of class leaders is to develop and strengthen the discipleship of the whole congregation, and each class should be as representative as possible of the full range of the membership.

2. *Special factors may govern the forming of classes if this facilitates the work of the class leader.*

There may well be special factors which make the assignment of certain members to a class leader more practicable or feasible: neighborhood groupings, for example, or familiarity with the leader in another setting, such as a Sunday school class or a Bible study group. The leaders' meeting should feel free to assign classes in this way—provided the special factors do not exclude anyone from such a class.

3. *Assign all new church members to a class leader.*

A good way to develop the office of class leader is to begin assigning all new members to a class when they join. As they take their membership vows and are welcomed into the fellowship of the church, their new class leader can stand with them, and be recognized by the congregation. It should be made clear on such occasions that class leaders are not the same as the "fellowship friends" or "Christian companions" with whom congregations often pair new church members for a few months to make them feel at home. Ministries of this nature are important, and should remain in place. The relationship with a class leader is very different, however, and the welcome extended to new members provides an opportunity for the pastor to inform the congregation accordingly.

4. *Invitations to join a class should be extended by class leaders in person.*

As the leaders' meeting determines the assignment of classes, invitations to join a class should be extended to each member by the class leader concerned.

Of course, there are bound to be refusals. However carefully the assignment process has taken into account the attitudes of prospective class members, there will be resistance, for any number of reasons. These refusals should be accepted graciously by the class leader, but without conceding the value and purpose of forming the classes—nor should the leader feel personally rejected. We are dealing here with the retuning of muscle in the church, the reactivation of that part of the body that gives it strength. As with all muscle that has not been used for a while, there will be resistance—and in due course, some aches and pains as well.

On the other hand, when a church member agrees to accept the invitation and join a class, the spiritual affirmation experienced by the leader is one of the highest privileges of the Christian life. The knowledge that someone else is willing to benefit from one's own walk with Christ, and the assurance that God's grace is indeed at work in the ministry and mission of the congregation, prove to be inestimable blessings.

Moreover, the forming of these classes marks the beginning of relationships that in many instances will last a lifetime. We know this for sure, because there are biographical accounts from our Methodist forebears that bear just such a testimony. (See the companion volume, *Class Leaders*.)

5. *Do not give up on members who are not initially receptive to the idea of having a class leader.*

As we have noted, it will take much advocacy and much persistence to inform and educate the congregations of today about the nature and purpose of class leaders and classes. Not only are there many Methodists who have no memory of class leaders; there are now many members of United Methodist congregations who were not originally Methodist.

The leaders' meeting should regularly discuss ways and means of extending the number of classes and class leaders. Invitations to join classes should be repeated, many times, and when least expected there will be a positive response. Likewise, every opportunity should be taken to show how class leaders are enriching the life and work of the congregation. At council and committee meetings, in Sunday school classes, and above all in the worship of the church, the office should be given visibility and affirmation.

Even so, there will be times when the congregation seems to be impervious, and the pilot process seems to be interminable. At such times, the leaders' meeting should be used to help leaders remember that they themselves have accepted the office, and are convinced that it is a means of grace. They have come to know that "watching over each other in love" is a method of forming faithful disciples and vital congregations, and that grace is indeed at work throughout the membership. As with all seed planted in good ground, it will be slower to grow than that which is planted in shallow ground. But it will also bear fruit when the other has long since withered (Matt. 13:3-8).

6. *Be open to the possibility of class meetings.*

While much has been made in this chapter of the contextual factors that make it unwise for class leaders in the average North American congregation to convene their classes as class meetings, this is not to say that such meetings should be avoided. On the contrary, the ideal situation for any large church would be for all members to meet regularly in a group to be accountable for their discipleship, and that all members would be willing to make the sort of commitment to be found in covenant discipleship groups. Such a church would be truly revolutionary—as indeed is the case in places where such discipleship is practiced.

As we noted in Part 1, the reality of the North American church is very far from this. In a large, inclusive, pluralistic church, only a few members are willing to make such a commitment. And in the present climate of individualism in North America, the great majority of church members will engage in group activities only to the extent that they themselves are helped. They are rarely willing to enter into Christian community as a means of improving their discipleship.

Even so, the reintroduction of class leaders can be an important step in this direction. At first, and for quite some time, classes will have to be regarded as a pastoral grouping of individuals, each member having a personal relationship with the class leader. But in due course, there may well be a desire on the part of some, or even all of the members, to have a meeting together, to share mutual experiences and to provide mutual support.

Class leaders should be ready for this opportunity, and should take full advantage of it. Suggestions for how to allow such class meetings to evolve are found in the companion volume, *Class Leaders*, along with other recommendations from branches of Methodism where the tradition of class meetings has been kept alive.

CLASS LEADERS AND OTHER CHURCH OFFICERS

Once they are introduced, a crucial aspect of the credibility of class leaders will be to clarify their relationship to other church leaders. Their direct link with the pastor, to say nothing of their appointment by charge conference, is sure to raise questions about the extent to which their responsibilities might duplicate or even conflict with those of other church officers.

The most important clarification is that class leaders provide a *complementary* role in the congregation. It is helpful in this regard to return to the distinction between transactional and transformational leadership we discussed in Chapter 7. Transactional leadership is responsible for meeting the needs of church members, and for the institutional maintenance of the church. Transformational leadership is responsible for keeping church members focused on the vision of the gospel and the obligations of their discipleship. This is not to say that these two leadership roles are mutually exclusive. Even the most fastidious chairperson of trustees can find a prophetic voice, and even the most visionary pastor has to deal with airconditioning. But it is to say that the two modes of leadership must be given distinct and equal emphasis in the life and work of the church.

We noted in Chapter 7 that in most congregations today the transactional mode of leadership predominates to the neglect of the transformational. Yet the answer to this imbalance does not lie in trying to make administrative and programmatic leaders more transformational. Their mode of leadership must be transactional, because they are responsible for running the church and meeting members' needs. Their energies are already expended in doing precisely that.

Class leaders, by contrast, have the freedom to function in a transformational mode. They are responsible for helping church members grow in their obedience to Jesus Christ. They are also responsible for directing them toward the resources they need in order to live out their discipleship in the world. In this way, they are fully complementary to the transactional leadership of the church.

On the one hand, class leaders need the administrative and programmatic dimensions of the congregation in order to resource their classes. Without these, the General Rule of Discipleship remains skeletal. On the other hand, they enrich the life and work of the congregation by involving their class members more intentionally in its ministry and mission. If there is any overlap, it is by way of reinforcing everyone else's work.

EX OFFICIO MEMBERSHIPS

This means that class leaders must not only be aware of everything that is going on in the programmatic life of the congregation: they must also be welcomed as significant new colleagues. It is recommended in the *Book of Discipline* that class leaders be *ex officio* members of the council on ministries or the administrative council. However, their leadership role will be greatly enhanced if all committees and task forces of the congregation invite a representative class leader to serve *ex officio* with them. And all leadership roles in the church will be further enhanced if other church officers will consult regularly with class leaders about their respective responsibilities.

Such a sharing of information and insights will have many advantages. To begin with, it will mutually enrich the leadership of the church. Class leaders will be better informed about opportunities for the involvement of their class members; and committees, commissions, and task forces will be better supported in their work. Likewise, class leaders will bring the insights of their classes to business and program meetings—classes that are widely representative of the congregation as a whole. In turn, they will impart to their class members a greater sense of involvement in the life and work of the larger church—a church that is not only connectional, but worldwide.

THE LAY LEADER AND CLASS LEADERS

In this regard, there is one church officer with whom class leaders should have an especially close relationship, and that is the lay leader of the congregation. The titles of the two offices are very similar, and it is important to keep them distinct in the life and work of the church. Yet they complement each other in very significant ways. The lay leader functions as the primary lay representative of the congregation, and has wide responsibilities for the fostering of lay ministry that will most effectively fulfill the church's mission. These responsibilities include membership on a number of key committees, and serving as interpreter to the congregation of the actions and programs of the general church.[52] The office of class leader, on the other hand, is more directly focused on helping a pastoral subgrouping of the congregation to be formed in Christian discipleship.

Because they complement one another so directly, it is essential to have good communication between the two. Accordingly, the lay leader should be an *ex officio* member of the monthly leaders' meeting. By attending these meetings, the lay leader can be better informed about the congregation as a whole, and at the same time contribute an overview of the congregation that will help the class leaders in their work. Since the two offices are distinct, there is nothing to prevent the lay leader from being a class leader as well; though few people are likely to have the time for both responsibilities.

THE MOST IMPORTANT WORD: RECOGNITION

In the final analysis, the most important word in the reintroduction of class leaders is *recognition:* recognition by the pastor that leaders in discipleship are there in the congregation, waiting to be asked to join in the pastoring of the flock; recognition by the congregation that some of their own members are called to be their leaders in following Christ; and recognition by the class leaders themselves that God's call to this leadership role is one of the highest privileges and responsibilities of the Christian life.

If all of this is recognized, by pastor and people alike, then class leaders will begin to assume their proper place in the congregation; and the preceding guidelines, while helpful perhaps at first, will quickly be left behind. For the office of class leader is not new. It was proven in practice by our Methodist forebears; it continues in practice among many of our Methodist colleagues; and it is still present in the collective memory of a church that badly needs the methodical discipleship it once nurtured.

The question to be asked, therefore, as a congregation considers incorporating the office of class leader into its life and work, is not whether it will work, but whether it is right. There are countless Methodists, past and present, who have answered that question with a resounding "yes." May there be many others who now decide to join them.

Conclusion
Christ All in All

The purpose of this volume has been to search out ways of forming faithful disciples in the church of today. To do this we have returned to the roots of Methodism, a movement first identified by its methodical approach to precisely this task: a discipleship that begins with surrender to Jesus Christ; a lifetime of continuing obedience to his teachings in the world under the guidance of the Holy Spirit; and a mutual accountability that watches over every member in love.

We have also sought ways in which the congregations of the church can be vital companies of faithful disciples who announce the good news of God's salvation to the world, and who live in the world as sign communities of God's coming reign of love and peace and justice. Vital congregations must be centered on Jesus Christ, so that every dimension of their life and work reflects the power and presence of the Holy Spirit.

The key to all of this is leadership: leaders in discipleship who can show each and every member of the church how to witness to Jesus Christ in the world, and how to follow his teachings through acts of compassion, justice, worship, and devotion, under the guidance of the Holy Spirit.

We have found that the Methodist tradition once again holds the answer: a weekly meeting to develop such leaders in a climate of accountability; and a time-honored office through which to implement their leadership. We have not copied all of this from our forebears, but have tried instead to do our homework, and to re-tradition their legacy. We have sought the genius of what they accomplished, and then adapted it for today in light of the scriptures and teachings of the church.

In so doing, we have been reminded that pursuit of these methods for their own sake will be self-defeating. A final word of warning is therefore in order. Covenant discipleship and class leaders are not models guaranteed to succeed simply because others have tried them and found that they work. There is only one way to faithful discipleship and congregational vitality, and that is for the church to be centered on Christ, and Christ alone—in our day and age, no less than that of our forebears. Any methods we adopt, any strategies, any goals or objectives must always give Christ center stage.

For only when Christ is honored by the leaders of the church, laity and clergy alike, can there be the oneness in the Holy Spirit that subsumes all differences and allows us a true foretaste of the coming reign of God, here on earth as in heaven:

> Christ, from whom all blessings flow,
> perfecting the saints below,
> hear us, who thy nature share,
> who thy mystic body are.
>
> Join us, in one spirit join,
> let us still receive of thine;
> still for more on thee we call,
> thou who fillest all in all.
>
> Move and actuate and guide,
> diverse gifts to each divide;
> placed according to thy will,
> let us all our work fulfill;
>
> Never from thy service move,
> needful to each other prove;
> use the grace on each bestowed,
> tempered by the art of God.
>
> Many are we now, and one,
> we who Jesus have put on;
> there is neither bond nor free,
> male nor female, Lord, in thee.
>
> Love, like death, hath all destroyed,
> rendered all distinctions void;
> names and sects and parties fall;
> thou, O Christ art all in all!

Charles Wesley[53]

Endnotes

1. The United Methodist Council of Bishops, *Vital Congregations—Faithful Disciples: Vision for the Church*. Foundation Document. Nashville: Graded Press, 1990, p. 10. Used by permission.

2. Ibid., p. 13.

3. Ibid., p. 119.

4. Juan Luis Segundo, *The Hidden Motives of Pastoral Action: Latin American Reflections* (Maryknoll: Orbis Books, 1978), p. 72.

5. I have addressed these questions in more detail in *God Does Not Foreclose: The Universal Promise of Salvation* (Nashville: Abingdon Press, 1990). See especially Chapter 4.

6. *The Bicentennial Edition of the Works of John Wesley, Volume 9: The Methodist Societies: History, Nature, and Design*, ed. Rupert E. Davies, (hereafter *Wesley's Works*) (Nashville: Abingdon Press, 1989), p. 69.

7. *Religion in America: 50 Years: 1935-1985*. The Gallup Report No. 236 (Princeton, NJ, 1985). This report has been revised and updated in *Religion in America: 1990 Report* (Princeton, NJ: The Princeton Religion Research Center, 1990). The trends remain the same.

8. *Gallup Report No. 236*, pp. 24-25.

9. See Robert E. Cushman, *Faith Seeking Understanding: Essays Theological and Critical* (Durham, NC: Duke University Press, 1981), pp. 243-55.

10. Frederick Herzog, *God-Walk: Liberation Shaping Dogmatics* (Maryknoll: Orbis Books, 1988).

11. *Wesley's Works*, 9:52. See also the *Covenant Discipleship Quarterly*, 1:3 (April 1986), p. 3.

12. *The United Methodist Hymnal: Book of United Methodist Worship* (Nashville: The United Methodist Publishing House, 1989), p. 26.

13. Juan Luis Segundo, *The Community Called Church* (Maryknoll: Orbis Books, 1973), pp. 78-86.

14. Jacques Ellul, *The Presence of the Kingdom* (New York: The Seabury Press, 1967), pp. 9-10.

15. Charles R. Taber, "God vs. Idols: A Model of Conversion," *Journal of the Academy for Evangelism in Theological Education*, Volume Three (1987-88), pp. 27-29.

16. Segundo, *Hidden Motives*, p. 72.

17. M. Douglas Meeks, *God the Economist: The Doctrine of God and Political Economy* (Minneapolis: Fortress Press, 1989), pp. 33-37.

18. A good example of this is the very positive response to *Disciple* Bible Study, launched in the late 1980s by The United Methodist Publishing House.

19. Stanley Hauerwas and William H. Willimon, *Resident Aliens: Life in the Christian Colony* (Nashville: Abingdon Press, 1989).

20. Dietrich Bonhoeffer, *The Cost of Discipleship* (New York: The Macmillan Co., 1960), p. 36.

21. John H. Leith, ed., *Creeds of the Churches: A Reader in Christian Doctrine from the Bible to the Present* (Atlanta: John Knox Press, 1973), pp. 7-8.

22. Orlando E. Costas, *Christ Outside the Gate: Mission Beyond Christendom* (Maryknoll: Orbis Books, 1982), pp. 174-87.

23. James W. Fowler, "John Wesley's Development in Faith," in *The Future of the Methodist Theological Traditions*, ed. M. Douglas Meeks (Nashville: Abingdon Press, 1985), pp. 172-92. See also James W. Fowler, *Stages of Faith: The Psychology of Human Development and the Quest for Meaning* (San Francisco: Harper and Row, 1981), p. 274.

24. *Disciple* Bible Study is published by The United Methodist Publishing House. *Walk to Emmaus* is resourced by The Upper Room. Literature for the other programs listed here can be obtained from Discipleship Resources, P.O. Box 189, Nashville, TN 37202, (615) 340-7284.

25. James D. Anderson and Ezra Earl Jones, *The Management of Ministry* (San Francisco: Harper and Row, 1978), p. 133.

26. Ibid., p. 131.

27. James D. Anderson and Ezra Earl Jones, *Ministry of the Laity* (San Francisco: Harper and Row, 1986), p. 19.

28. *Wesley's Works*, 19:258 and 9:529.

29. Ibid., 9:70.

30. Ibid., 9:272.

31. Ibid., 9:273.

32. Ibid.

33. Ibid.

34. Anderson and Jones, *Ministry of the Laity*, p. 19.

35. *The Book of Discipline of The United Methodist Church, 1988* (Nashville: The United Methodist Publishing House, 1988), para. 268.

36. *The History of American Methodism,* gen.ed. Emory Stevens Bucke, 3 vols. (Nashville: Abingdon Press, 1964), 3:467.

37. For example: John Miley, *Treatise on Class Meetings* (Cincinnati, Ohio, 1854); L. Rosser, *Class Meetings* (Richmond, Virginia, 1855); Charles L. Goodell, *The Drillmaster of Methodism: Principles and Methods for the Class Leader and Pastor* (New York, 1902).

38. Ernst Troeltsch, *The Social Teaching of the Christian Churches,* 2 vols. (Chicago: University of Chicago Press, 1976), 2:461-62.

39. *Book of Discipline,* pp. 74-77.

40. *Wesley's Works,* 9:263.

41. *Wesley's Works,* 2:90.

42. *Book of Discipline,* para. 248.

43. For example, Duane A. Ewers, *A Ministry of Caring;* and Herbert Mather, *Planning a Shepherding Program for Your Congregation.* Both were published by Discipleship Resources.

44. *Book of Discipline,* para. 268.2.

45. Ibid., para. 246.7.

46. Ibid., para. 404.3.

47. For some examples of Methodist literature suitable for this purpose, see the companion volume, *Class Leaders.* See also the references to class leaders in ·*Wesley's Works, Volume 9.*

48. *Wesley's Works,* 5:405.

49. See, for example, *The Doctrines and Discipleship of the Methodist Episcopal Church, 1936,* para. 571.2.; and *The Doctrines and Discipleship of the Methodist Episcopal Church, South, 1938,* para.152.

50. Orlando E. Costas, *Christ Outside the Gate,* pp. 79-80.

51. See J.A. Leatherman, "The Decline of the Class Meeting," in *Spiritual Renewal for Methodism,* ed. Samuel Emerick (Nashville: Methodist Evangelistic Materials, 1958), p. 46.

52. *Book of Discipline, 1988,* para.251.

53. *The United Methodist Hymnal,* #550.

Resources

All of the following are available from: **Discipleship Resources, P.O. Box 189, Nashville, TN 37202-0189 • (615)340-7284.**

Covenant Discipleship: Christian Formation through Mutual Accountability by David Lowes Watson.

This new manual advances the guidelines for covenant discipleship groups by incorporating learnings of the past decade from groups in the United States and around the world. **(#DR091B)**

Class Leaders: Recovering a Tradition by David Lowes Watson.

Taking the later Methodist class meeting as a model, this book shows how class leaders can foster the discipleship of a pastoral subdivision of the congregation. **(#DR092B)**

Forming Christian Disciples: The Role of Covenant Discipleship and Class Leaders in the Congregation by David Lowes Watson.

This third volume gives the procedures for introducing and sustaining covenant discipleship groups, and explains the role of class leaders in the congregation. **(#DR093B)**

These three books are available individually or as a set: the *Covenant Discipleship Trilogy.* **(#M302P)**

Covenants on Campus: Covenant Discipleship Groups for College and University Students by Kim Hauenstein-Mallet and Kenda Creasy Dean.

Written especially for campus ministers, college-town church leaders, and college students, this book explains the values of shared Christian discipleship according to biblical principles. **(#DR099B)**

Branch Groups: Covenant Discipleship for Youth by Lisa Grant.

An adaptation of the early Methodist class meeting for the youth of today, branch groups enable young people to practice the basics of discipleship in covenant with one another. **(#DR067B)**

The Early Methodist Class Meeting: Its Origins and Significance by David Lowes Watson. Foreword by Albert C. Outler.

This volume provides the historical background of the early class meeting, including a theological assessment of its place in Wesley's leadership of the Methodist movement. **(#DR017B)**

Wesley Speaks on Christian Vocation by Paul Wesley Chilcote.

Using Wesley's own writings as a source of inspiration, Chilcote addresses the deep vocational questions that shape the life of the faithful Christian disciple. **(#DR041B)**

Discípulos Responsables por David Lowes Watson. Prólogo por Mortimer Arias.

Este libro presenta una excelente base para la formación, desarrollo, y acción de grupos de discípulos responsables en nuestra iglesia. **(#F023B)**

Discovering the Modern Methodists

This video resource on two cassettes features David Lowes Watson in four presentations:
- The Need for Muscle in the Church
- The Dynamics of Discipleship
- The Early Methodist Class Meeting
- Covenant Discipleship Groups

Each presentation is 20 minutes long, with an accompanying leader's guide for a further 30 minutes of discussion. **(#M301VC)**

Christian Formation Binder

This vinyl three-ring binder is designed to hold copies of the *Covenant Discipleship Quarterly,* the *Journal for Covenant Discipleship,* and resources and materials for the use of class leaders in their work. **(#M303M)**

Christian Formation Brochure

Copies of this brochure are available for distribution in congregations and other settings, and may be purchased in multiples of 100. **(#M299L)**

Covenant Discipleship Quarterly

Available in English and Spanish, the *Quarterly* is an important supplement to the handbook, *Covenant Discipleship.* It features articles about Christian discipleship in different contexts, and reports from covenant discipleship groups around the world.

Journal for Covenant Discipleship

The *Journal,* with a separate page for each week of the year, provides a place for group members to record their experiences and insights, enabling them to give a more meaningful account of their discipleship at their weekly meetings.

Both the *Quarterly* and the *Journal* can be ordered from the **Office of Covenant Discipleship and Christian Formation, General Board of Discipleship, P.O. Box 840, Nashville, TN 37202-0840. (615) 340-7010.**